ELITE

Uncovering Classism in Unitarian Universalist History

Mark W. Harris

D1362190

Skinner House Books

Boston

Printed in the United States

Cover design by Suzanne Morgan
Text design by Jeff Miller

ISBN 1-55896-573-4
978-1-55896-573-7
eBook version: 978-1-55896-607-9

6 5 4 3 2 1
13 12 11 10

Library of Congress Cataloging-in-Publication Data

Harris, Mark W.
    Elite : uncovering classism in Unitarian Universalist history / Mark Harris.
        p. cm.
    Includes bibliographical references and index.
    ISBN-13: 978-1-55896-573-7 (pbk. : alk. paper)
    ISBN-10: 1-55896-573-4 (pbk. : alk. paper)
1. Christian sociology—Unitarian Universalist Association—History. 2. Unitarian Universalist Association—Membership—History. 3. Christian sociology—United States—History. 4. Classism—United States—History. 5. United States—Church history. I. Title.
    BX9833.H37 2011
    289.1'3208620973—dc22

                                                                    2010032148

Contents

Introduction

WHEN I TELL fellow Unitarian Universalists that I serve the First Parish of Watertown, Massachusetts, they are sometimes surprised and generally respond incredulously, "I never knew there was a UU church there."

Unitarian Universalists often assume that UU congregations belong in wealthy suburbs where the grass is greener and the children go to high-achieving schools. This assumption exists alongside the half-defensive, half-optimistic ideology of genuine diversity. Until recently, Watertown was urban, industrial, and populated by working class immigrants. While it is still densely populated, its proximity to Boston has helped the real estate market put a Watertown address out of the price range for most working class people today. Yet one colleague said that his parishioners would consider Watertown a ghetto. This is a minister who would preach that our faith is for all people and should appeal to diverse populations. No wonder we feel confused. I wrote this book because I have been plagued by the need to understand where Unitarian Universalism flourishes and who sits in our pews—and why.

We assume that our Unitarian ancestors were almost all wealthy Boston blue bloods. We also assume that all our Universalist ancestors were poor country bumpkins. Although these stereotypes are not entirely accurate, perhaps some of us still want to believe that we are somehow an elite group of people who had a privileged past, at least on the Unitarian side. We say we aspire to be democratic and inclusive, but we are comforted by our litany of influential and prestigious forebears. Many Unitarian Universalists are torn between who is actually sitting in our pews and who we wish was sitting there. Do we really want multicultural communities and diverse churches? This book looks primarily at historically who has been attracted to our Unitarian and Universalist faiths in order to help UUs today consider where we are going in the new millennium.

The First Parish of Watertown is an ancient parish, one of the five oldest congregations in the Unitarian Universalist Association. It was founded in 1630 by Puritan Englishmen who stated in their covenant that they were escaping "the pollutions of the world" to "bring forth our intentions into actions." This band of white Anglo-Saxon Protestants and their descendants helped form many congregations that eventually became the nucleus of an established church, whose membership exerted enormous economic, political, social, and educational influence in Massachusetts. These congregations were part of the first embodiment of what Leonard Silk and Mark Silk refer to as "The American Establishment" in their book of that title. The Watertown church was one of the founding congregations of Harvard College, and every year I receive an invitation to march in the commencement procession with the president of Harvard. The church has been home to members of the Coolidge family; the radical Unitarian minister Theodore Parker; George Curtis, a chief justice of the U.S. Supreme Court; and Lydia Maria Child, the abolitionist remembered for her Thanksgiving song, "Over the River and

Through the Wood." Other members included business leaders, artists, authors, and other cultural and societal movers and shakers. Then Watertown had an enormous population shift. Everything changed.[1]

In the mid-nineteenth century, the demographic character of Watertown, like other WASP communities, was transformed. First, the population began to swell with laborers for the Watertown Arsenal, many of whom were victims of the Irish potato famine. Then Italians were added to the new ethnic mix. Soon wave after wave of Armenians fleeing the Turkish genocide found employment at the Hood Rubber factory. A substantial Greek population joined them, and Orthodox churches started to appear on the landscape. As Watertown became more industrial and urban, its most venerable institution, the Unitarian Church, began to decline. The values of diversity and inclusiveness that UUs celebrate today did not exist in the mid-twentieth century. Unitarians led the march to the suburbs.

By 1966, when Rev. David Rankin was called to serve his first congregation, he found an "old gray ghost" atop the rising knoll on Watertown's Church Street, with twelve to fourteen people attending the worship services. Almost every aspect of church life had disintegrated.

In an unprecedented action by Unitarian standards, Rankin went door to door, giving literature to six thousand families and talking to hundreds about the liberal message of Unitarian Universalism. This evangelical approach worked, at least temporarily. Former Unitarians came back to church, along with ex-Catholics and even a Muslim. Yet it was not enough to save their Gothic edifice, especially after Rankin moved on. The small congregation simply could not support two large buildings—a meeting house and a parish hall. The walls of the meeting house had holes, and the floorboards gave way when walked upon. In 1975 it was torn down, and the congregation moved next door to the parish hall, where it eventually grew and today flourishes. At least for now, the congregation is assured of a continuing existence.

In "Good News," a sermon delivered in 1968, Rankin cited population shifts and an "anti-city bias" among the reasons for the decline and death of UU churches in cities, but he also observed that in suburban communities the liberal churches were holding their own or growing. Rankin closed his sermon with the good news that "an ancient parish has been revived. A new vision is being found."[2]

This book asks Unitarian Universalists to evaluate Rankin's new vision. We need to examine the problem that Rankin addressed nearly a half century ago and ask why we are still facing these concerns. How can we in our denominational life find a model for church renewal that will truly reflect the diversity we say we want in our faith? That faith says we believe that people of every race, class, color, and sexual orientation are welcome. We preach openness to diversity in theology, culture, and identity—but where are all those people who represent this diversity in America? They are not sitting in our stackable chairs.

Rev. Tom Schade delivered a sermon "Hoping Their Hopes" at the First Unitarian Church of Worcester, Massachusetts in March 2010, suggesting that every church community is "working through one central issue." For his congregation that issue was: How should well-educated, sophisticated, and generally prosperous people conduct their religious lives in the changing circumstances of Worcester? Worcester is generally perceived as a working class, industrial city. Yet the type of people Schade finds at his church reflect a different socio-economic and educational reality.[3] The church may be in a mixed community, yet the membership generally reflects the upper-middle class. And it didn't happen by design.

Does the Unitarian Universalist faith only appeal to a narrow segment of the population—a liberal, economically comfortable, well-educated elite—or is that simply a self-fulfilling prophesy? Most of us do not personally know people who live in poverty. If like attracts like, then reaching out to more diverse populations might mean that we would have to change and adapt. Can we do that?

John Hurley, the director of communications at the UUA quoted Robert Cummins in an address given at the 150th anniversary celebration of the First Universalist Church of Minneapolis. In 1943, Cummins, the Universalist General Superintendent, said the Universalist church should be a place "where all are welcome: colored and colorless." How do we achieve that dream? Hurley referred to the UUA 2007 General Assembly resolution on "Truth, Repair and Reconciliation," which reminds us that learning our history can help us heal from painful stories in our past. We cannot address that which remains hidden or unspoken. And as Hurley notes, some of this uncovered history of oppression and exclusion comes at the "intersection of race and class."[4] We need to know these stories in order to challenge the stereotypes about who belongs among us, and stop assuming that we can only appeal to certain people—especially if we are committed to creating a just world.

My interest in class issues began nearly forty years ago. At that time I was a graduate student in history working on a thesis about my home town of New Salem, Massachusetts. In the process, I began a journey that led me to the ministry. I discovered two faiths, Unitarianism and Universalism. Both affirmed the use of reason in interpreting the Bible, a loving God who embraced all, and an understanding that human nature was basically good. I juxtaposed my new faith against a childhood religion that taught me a literal understanding of the Bible stories, a judging God who filled me with unending guilt, and a sinful human nature that really could not do anything right or worthy in God's eyes until Jesus saved me. Leaving my childhood faith was easy. I soon came to believe that living out my new faith and sharing it with others was what I was meant to do with my life, and so it has been ever since.

More pertinent to the theme of this book was another thesis I worked on at the University of New Hampshire about the decline and failure of rural Unitarianism. The central reason why rural Unitarianism failed was that its rational, intellectual faith could not speak to plain, rural folk who needed something other than intellectualism to address their religious needs. Indeed, when I served my first church in the poor New England mill town of Palmer, Massachusetts, a respected colleague with a long Unitarian pedigree told me that my church was only there for historical reasons—the denomination would never start a new UU church in a place like that. It did not fit that stereotype of a green, leafy, rich suburb filled with smart people.

I was raised in one of those places where Unitarianism failed. I served in another place where it was assumed it would fail. Now I once again find myself in a place that is consigned to the UU scrap heap. Rural villages, mill towns, and industrial cities are where, we're told, only uneducated buffoons, the working poor, or ethnic groups live. These places are not home to smart, cultured liberals like us. The population is not our kind.

My thesis on rural Unitarianism forced me to reflect upon the question: Can liberal religion appeal to all classes of people? Ever since my former colleague looked at my church and said, you don't belong among us, you are not one of us, I have longed to write this book. This is an attempt to respond to the stereotype that we must have a certain pedigree, education, or profession to be Unitarian Universalists.

I have also wondered about class differences on a personal level. My father was a rags-to-riches success story. He spent his childhood living on welfare during the depression after his father's business failed. He used to tell the story of standing in a welfare line for shoes and having to procure two pairs because his brother was too embarrassed to stand with him. I enjoyed the benefits of money growing up, but our family values were pure working class. I became the educated "idiot" my father both wanted and feared. My education assigns me to a certain class today, but I have often felt confused. With whom do I belong?

Those who promote a stereotype that we must attract a certain type of person in a certain kind of town do us no favors. I first thought UUs were those people who had it made and never had to struggle with anything. As a minister, I have learned that rich and poor, educated by traditional measures or not, all have religious needs that we can respond to.

We don't talk about class very much in Unitarian Universalist circles, giving far more time and energy to race. Class is a hard subject to talk about because many of us grew up believing that

America has no class structure, or that most everyone is middle class, or that even if you are poor, we are still all created equal, and you, too, can grow up to be president of the United States. We sometimes say we are all getting richer or that everyone has an equal chance to succeed. Yet in many ways class is the most important predictor of what kind of opportunities someone will have in life. We are stratified financially, socially, and educationally in ways predicted by class. A minister is upper-middle class by virtue of education, even if he or she does not make much money. Unitarian Universalists say they want to work toward greater equality by creating a multicultural and multiracial faith. But how do we do that with respect to class if our racial and cultural diversity all comes from the same socio-economic group? Then again, perhaps it doesn't. We may be more diverse than we think, and accept the elite stereotype to evoke liberal guilt.

The essential question is: Who belongs with us? Sometimes Unitarian Universalists believe the stereotype that we are only educated suburbanites, when it is clearly not true. My wife grew up as one of six children in a family that struggled to survive economically, yet she is a born UU and so is her mother. Many Unitarian Universalists live in marginal economic circumstances or do not have college educations. I believe that at heart Unitarian Universalists long to have a faith that learns from all kinds of people, rich and poor. I never want to feel there is anyone, including myself, who does not belong.

In a 2009 report, Starr King School for the Ministry President Rebecca Parker quotes seven areas the school works toward. One is: "Broaden Unitarian Universalist identity to include racial and cultural expressions of Unitarian and Universalist values, countering a history of Unitarian Universalist enmeshment with white privilege and economic privilege that limits Unitarian Universalism's accessibility and hospitality to many for whom its strengths could be life-giving."[5] This vision of a democratic, open faith for all kinds of people has long been part of our expressed dreams, but we have never been able to make this vision manifest.

That is why I wrote this book. I started with my own home town and family shadows. Most of this book contains what I discovered about the shadows of my faith community. Now I want to use that journey to call us to a faith that can be shared among all classes of people. Perhaps Unitarian Universalism is a thinking person's faith, but we can find thinking people in all classes and stripes of society. Perhaps we will learn that not all genuine thought leads to the same conclusion. We can *all* learn and change when we find ways to reach out to others.

Margaret Fuller, a leading Transcendentalist who is sometimes called America's first feminist, once wrote to her Unitarian father, "Your reluctance to go 'among strangers' cannot too soon be overcome; & the way to overcome it, is not to remain *at home*, but to go among them and resolve to *deserve* & obtain the love & esteem of those, who have never before known you. With them you have a fair opportunity to *begin the world anew* . . ."[6]

Our theology says this vision to "begin the world anew" must be with all kinds of people, not just with the social circle we create or like-minded liberals. It must be practiced in an ever-intentional manner and in ever-widening circles if our faith is going to be truly transformational. Perhaps this is how Unitarian Universalism can fulfill its democratic vision, and become more than a faith for a few.

The British Challenge and
American Beginnings

THE MOVIE BIOGRAPHY *Miss Potter*, starring Renee Zell-weger as Beatrix Potter, includes a scene in which Beatrix is entertaining Norman Warne of the Frederick Warne Publishing Company. Norman is given the task of working with Beatrix on her bunny book. He eventually becomes her suitor as well, much to the dismay of Beatrix's mother, who is a social climber and a snob. She despises Norman's presence in her home and in the film remarks to her daughter, "I wish you wouldn't invite tradespeople into the house. They carry dust."

A reviewer of the film, Anthony Lane, commented in the *New Yorker* that those like Mrs. Potter, who were trying to climb to the top of the social ladder, would not wish to marry off their children to someone who was halfway up. Lane then adds some pertinent information that isn't provided by the movie. Despite Mrs. Potter's clawing for upper class pretensions, the Potters would never be accepted on the highest rungs. At one point in the film, Beatrix reminds her father that their family money comes from the print-ing factories and that they are only two generations removed from being tradespeople.[1]

Although the Potters' wealth qualified them as upper-middle class, their regional background and religious affiliations excluded them from social acceptance among the most fashionable London society. They were cut off by their faith. They were Unitarians. Potter's biographer, Linda Lear, writes that the "family's strong identification with Unitarianism accounted for a certain social isolation."[2] Beatrix underscored this when she commented that in London society, some family friends were in "a different light, we in none at all."[3]

Those most familiar with the history of New England Unitarianism may be surprised at the cultural snobbery toward Unitarianism in England, exemplified by the plight of the Potters. In New England, the Unitarian faith developed within the Standing Order of Congregational Churches. Many present-day Unitarian Universalist congregations at one time embodied this establishment. They were the makers of the social order. In Britain, the Unitarian faith developed outside the establishment among those led by the dissenting clergy, who refused to subscribe to the Act of Uniformity and were forced to leave the church of England in 1662 as part of the Great Ejection.

The history of Unitarianism in Britain is complicated because it has many roots—Presbyterian, Baptist, Methodist, Independent, and, in its organizational beginnings, even a disaffected Anglican, Theophilus Lindsey. In 1772, more than a century after the Great Ejection, the first avowed Unitarian church held its initial service. More decades passed before Unitarianism became legal in 1813. While other dissenters could worship somewhat freely after 1689 with the passage of the Toleration Act, the liberals were excluded because they did not teach the correct doctrines. All of the dissenters after 1662 had to fight for the right to worship and hope they would not lose their property if they were caught.

Twice I have served short-term ministries at Underbank Chapel in Stannington, near Sheffield, England. Underbank is in glorious country on the edge of the Peak District National Park and literally sits under the bank off the edge of the road. It dates from 1652 as a congregation, but its first pastor, Isaac Darwent, was among those ejected in 1662, as was the parish priest in the central city of Sheffield. Darwent was subject to the Five Mile Act, which meant that he could not come within five miles of his former parish or he would be subject to prosecution—a vigorous religious restraining order. The British government also seized the property of dissenters and forced them to meet in secret.[4]

Unitarians in England also endured a physical, spatial aspect to the prejudice against them. In the center of Sheffield sits Upper Chapel, a wonderful building constructed in 1700, but the visitor has to go through an alley to enter the gates to find this hidden building. The same is true of another congregation I served in England, Rosslyn Hill Chapel in London. Set back from the street and not visible to the average passerby, the original building, built in 1692, looks like a brick function hall, which is how it is used now. It is almost the opposite of our New England parish churches, where Puritans often chose the highest ground in town for their church, so it would be the symbol of a shining city for all to see, the moral compass for the entire community.

After 1689 dissenting groups could meet legally in Britain—but not the Unitarians. Many of the chapels that later became Unitarian were officially Presbyterian or Congregational in the 1600s and 1700s. They were best served by not being too conspicuous as to their purpose. Graham and Judy Hague, the authors of the architectural history *The Unitarian Heritage*, tell us that "the homely, domestic architecture of these chapels reflects both the modest standing of their members and their fear of persecution." They needed protective cover.

Until the eighteenth century, churches almost always had the medieval character of chancels, high altars, and stained glass. These new meeting houses were more like houses with barns attached, but now they became chapel and minister's residence.[5] The kind of symbolic power over the community that was true in New England never existed for the dissenters, especially the Unitarians, in Britain. They met five miles away from the parish boundary or gathered in secret, hiding from the authorities—or at the least they met in very humble circumstances.

In many ways, the Potters reflect the class status among the British Unitarians as a whole. Not being Anglican, nonconformists were denied access to the universities. Thus, a tradition of dissenting academies began after 1662, and since ejected clergy had to earn a living, many of them tutored students privately. The academies often evolved into institutions marked by superior scholarship. They encouraged freedom of inquiry, used new learning methods, and emphasized the sciences.[6] Education became central to the Unitarians. The most famous British Unitarian, Joseph Priestley, believed that knowledge is power.

The Unitarians became the vanguard of a new middle class. They were aspiring, independent folk, who wanted to overcome the religious and civil prejudices they had encountered. Ruth Watts says that the "Unitarians came almost completely from the middle-class to artisan sections of society."[7] During the nineteenth century, the number of wealthier industrialists and intelligentsia gradually increased. Even though Unitarians were not allowed to receive the traditional university education that would lead to a learned profession, they found other avenues to success. Many Unitarians entered the business world and achieved success as entrepreneurs.

Andrea Greenwood, in a paper on "British Unitarianism, Education, and Class," says that in Britain the Unitarians were an aspiring middle class, not a wealthy upper class. If they eventually owned the factories in Britain, they worked their way up the ladder to do so. No one typifies this more than Josiah Wedgwood. Today, we may think of Wedgwood as synonymous with fine china, but when he started his pottery works, he had few prospects for success. Wedgwood was born to an impoverished potter's family and needed to work hard merely to survive. His response to his inauspicious origins was to create an industry by gaining a practical, scientific understanding of how to use paints, glazes, and firing processes that would enable him to succeed.

Moreover, he did not treat his workers the way factory owners in America did because his religious values had cost him a place in society, not afforded him one. So he was known for providing running water for workers to wash themselves and allowing time for lunch and family life. Wedgwood wanted his workers to have safer and more pleasant conditions, including the highest standards of ventilation at the time.

Wedgwood learned many of his innovations from his partner, Thomas Whieldon. These included the renting of accommodations to workers, fair wages, and the bonus of a pair of shoes or a shirt. Wedgwood apparently taught fair-mindedness to his son Tom, who found himself annoyed by the wealthy customers. He said that he had been brought up too long "to feel equal to every-

body, to bear the haughty manner of those who come into a shop."
While Wedgwood's views on industry's benevolence to workers
was genuine and heartfelt, Jenny Uglow, author of *The Lunar
Men*, says that he was also "blinkered" by how much exploitation
existed.[8]

The distinction between the factory owners who had to work
their way to the top and those who did not is reflected in a phrase
relayed by one of my former parishioners in Milton, a wealthy
Boston suburb. He said that in Milton, the Unitarians don't work,
they make money. Wedgwood was a Unitarian who worked, at
least until he achieved success and a marked degree of status.

Joseph Priestley understood that Unitarians were at a great
disadvantage religiously and politically. In her book *Gender, Power
and the Unitarians in England, 1760–1860*, Ruth Watts says that
Priestley "emphasized the necessity for civil liberty, that is, the
rights of all to freedom of conscience, education, and religion, and
saw no need for an established church." He "disliked the aristocracy and hereditary power, preferring the morality and capabilities
of the middle classes." As a result, Priestley wanted all careers to
be open to talent rather than hierarchy and privilege. Eventually
Priestley's radical theology, which equaled his radical politics and
his support for the French Revolution, with its "liberty, equality,
and fraternity" motto, resulted in his exile from England after an
unruly mob burned his house, laboratory, and the Unitarian
churches in Birmingham.

Upon arrival in America, Priestley chose to live in relatively
tolerant Pennsylvania, a haven for the Quakers, another group
which had suffered persecution. In Pennsylvania, Priestley was not
the outcast he would have been in Boston. In New England, the

once-persecuted Puritans had become the establishment and the liberal wing of that established church preferred to keep their Unitarian religious views hidden so as not to upset the uniform control of the state church. The New England religious liberals advocated order over liberty and feared being labeled political or theological radicals.[9]

This history is highlighted in *Joseph Priestley and English Unitarianism in America* by J. D. Bowers. Bowers quotes a letter from James Taylor, a minister in Philadelphia and a board member of the American Unitarian Association, to Ezra Stiles Gannett, who was William Ellery Channing's associate at the Federal Street Church and the secretary of the American Unitarian Association. Taylor noted that English "Unitarianism finds little favor among the rich, the fashionable, & those who are immersed in the concerns of an extensive business; it has much greater attractions for persons in comparatively humble life, & of unpretending manners, who love to cultivate their understandings, preferring the improvement of the mind to the gratification of the senses. . . ."[10] Bowers says that Taylor was upset about the Brahmin status of New England Unitarianism, along with its theological exclusivity, where the Socinian or human view of Jesus that Priestley and the English Unitarians professed was too radical for the Bostonians— who were almost all Arians, believing that Jesus was a divine being, but not part of the Trinity or coequal with God.

Further developments within Unitarianism in Britain reflected class conflict. Unitarianism grew by the addition of smaller groups which often had their own theological divisions. General Baptists believed that salvation was open to all rather than a particular few. For a time they were associated with Universalism but then became part of the Unitarian fold. The Universalist leaders, Richard Wright and William Vidler, believed in a more aggressive evangelical style than was typical for non-proselytizing Unitarians.

The Methodist Unitarians, led by Joseph Cooke, were of a different socio-economic class than most Unitarians. They are described as "weavers, warpers, wool-sorters, overlookers, hatters, cloggers, and shoemakers, who sought redress for their economic oppression in the radical reform movements of the day."[11] Some of them were socialists and active in the formation of cooperatives. Their chapel in Rochdale was called the "Coop Chapel." They officially became part of the Unitarian movement in 1844.

John Relly Beard joined William Gaskell, the husband of the famous writer Elizabeth Gaskell, to form the Unitarian Home Missionary Board in 1854. They advocated for a more evangelical, popular faith that would appeal to thinking, working class folk and have domestic missions in poorer neighborhoods of industrial cities. Beard became involved in the education of the working class and advocated for greater opportunities for all ranks and ages. He wished for all to gain economic power. The board established missions in several cities, including Liverpool, and new congregations for the unchurched working poor. Mary Carpenter was involved in the Domestic Mission in Bristol and helped set up a Ragged School to serve poor inner city children. Watts notes that while the Unitarians worked hard to broaden education opportunities for all, their efforts had an underlying paternalism. They were certain, she says, of their own enlightenment.[12]

This effort to create a wider constituency had mixed success and contributed to a split within Unitarian ranks between those who wanted to be more explicitly sectarian and those who did not.

In 1853 Manchester New College moved to London, which helped prompt the formation of a new training school by the Unitarian Home Missionary Board in the north of England. The new institution became a threat to some because of its avowed mission of "training ministers suited to the wants of the less educated classes." Its goal "aims at training those who shall be fitted to labour among the poor to speak to the 'common people' and to bring Unitarian Christianity to the hearts and homes of the great mass of society." The founders concluded that Unitarianism had failed to address the needs of poorer families and a more diverse ministry could be more responsive to the growing needs of congregations.

During the discussions about moving the college to London, the widely influential James Martineau argued that no one expected Unitarians to "exercise a wide influence over the uneducated masses of English society." Instead Martineau wanted to influence highbrow culture and the more intellectually advanced people of the age. He argued against competing with "the popular sects."[13]

These divergent views led to a split between the two factions in the Unitarian movement, resulting in two theological schools, one in London (eventually moving to Oxford) and the other in Manchester; two rival newspapers; and two hymnbooks. A joke told at the time was that the movement had two wings but never managed to get off the ground. So this divisiveness rooted in class and identity prevented the movement from ever having the chance to flourish.[14]

From its very beginning, Unitarianism in Britain wedded radical theology with politics. Unitarians were consistent critics of government policies and advocates of reform—especially in education but also in economic policies and women's rights. Anna

Barbauld, the writer and wife of the minister at Rosslyn Hill in London, spoke out against the declaration of war against France. She said that the British government behaved like "animals of prey." She was scandalized by the fact that the army could "desolate a country," and "destroy the fair face of nature," and that the country's leaders had the impiety to call upon God "to assist us in it."[15] The Unitarian opposition to the war and affirmation of France led to their being labeled *Jacobins*—for the radical French club known for its support of the French Revolution's left-wing politics. Unitarians found the French Revolution especially appealing because it removed the yoke of an established church.

The most distinguishing feature of the British Unitarians was their unrelenting attacks on the establishment. Once he had been driven out of the country, Priestley could make the following report about America:

> Happily in this country, the church has no alliance with the state, every person being allowed to worship God in whatever manner he pleases, or not worship him at all, if he be not so disposed, without being liable to any civil disobedience. In these circumstances, truth has the best chance of being heard. . . .[16]

Unfortunately, Priestley discovered an establishment in New England that had its own ideas about truth, as disseminated through the societal control of the Standing Order.

In *The Social Sources of Denominationalism*, theologian H. Richard Niebuhr maintained that people tend to choose a faith based on social status or class. He wrote, "The religion of the untutored and economically disenfranchised classes has distinct ethical and psychological characteristics, corresponding to the needs of these groups." The poor shun "ethical and intellectual sophistication" in favor of emotional spontaneity and energy of religious feeling. Millennialism promises tangible goods to them, and by seeking salvation, they hope to reverse their present status in the social structure of the community. The early liberals, or Arminians, in New England offered a more secular, rational approach, and this is reflected in the adherents to that faith.[17] They were generally also among the more financially secure, as those who placed their energy on improving their lot in this life became less focused on the other world, where the gift of God's grace would secure them a place in heaven. The Arminians also placed a greater emphasis on the individual's ability to play a part in his or her own salvation. While Calvinists waited for God's grace to fill them, liberals increasingly placed an emphasis on their own good works as a pathway to heaven. Economic and educational success were sure signs of their idea of salvation.

Some liberal religious tendencies in New England prior to 1740 were fomented by increased economic and commercial success, especially along the seaboard. New church members were recognized more openly, especially with the implementation of the Half-Way Covenant, a device that allowed nonmembers to have their children baptized.

The greatest divisions within the churches surfaced when the Great Awakening affected congregations throughout the region. This new spirit of revivalism resulted in a four-part division of the Congregational clergy and their parishioners in New England. The group closest to the revival were the "New Lights," who wanted to extend Calvinism. This group included a radical element, whose style was flamboyant and evangelical, as well as more vindictive toward the establishment. The "New Lights" were predominately Yale graduates with greatest influence in Connecticut and rural Massachusetts.

"Old Lights" dominated the middle ground. These were moderate Calvinists who wanted to preach plain, profitable divinity without disturbing the established system. Like the "New Lights," the "Old Lights" had a radical wing. These were the Arminians, or liberals, who were a decidedly anti-revival group. Arminian churches often grew where there was a large, heterogeneous population that did not desire a defined theological position. Arminian ministers were more willing to exchange pulpits. They wanted people to experience a variety of viewpoints. Orthodox preachers often did not want to exchange because they felt the liberals were preaching heresy.

The greatest liberal leaders in the eighteenth century were Charles Chauncy, Ebenezer Gay, and Jonathan Mayhew, all of whom opposed the revival. Chauncy, minister of the First Church, Boston, believed that "an enlightened Mind, not raised Affections ought always to be the Guide of those who call themselves Men." This was the way to "saving knowledge."[18] The liberals shunned a theological style that reflected a quick, emotional conversion to salvation in favor of a slow, educational process devoted to the conduct of life. Alan Heimert, the author of *Religion and the American Mind*, felt that Chauncy, who had led the published response against the revival with his book *Seasonable Thoughts*, took this educational view of salvation so seriously that his concept of heaven resembled a glorified Harvard graduate school, where the best and the brightest belong. Here he would be the dean to his colleagues who had already received their doctorates on earth.

Heimert offers a revisionist understanding of the traditional view that those who were liberalizing theology were political liberals as well. He writes,

> It has long been received historical doctrine that "Liberal" religion—the rationalism espoused by critics of Awakening enthusiasm and further developed as a counterthrust to eighteenth-century Calvinism—was comparatively humane and progressive in outlook and import, that, indeed, liberal religion prepared the way for a revolution of which its spokesmen were the heralds. It is my conclusion, however, that Liberalism was profoundly conservative, politically as well as socially, and that its leaders, insofar as they did in fact embrace the Revolution, were the most reluctant of rebels.[19]

He says that while many of the liberals were committed patriots during the American Revolution, they were never committed democrats.

In his book on America's religious awakenings, William McLoughlin says that while liberals preached that all people had the gift of reason to understand the laws of nature and God, they also believed that God gave these gifts in differing amounts. He writes, "Birth, intelligence, and education distinguished the *aristoi*, the best and wisest, from *hoi polloi*."[20]

The liberal Jonathan Mayhew, often thought to be the closest thing to a theological Unitarian in the eighteenth century, as well as being a strong proponent of revolution, said that the common people were intellectually limited. In his sermon "Christian sobriety," Mayhew wondered which we should desire in society: the wise and knowing few who can judge things according to truth and propriety or "the multitude of fools and madmen." This ignorant rabble, according to Mayhew, "had neither skill, taste, nor judgment."[21]

Mayhew was so radical in his theology that most of his future colleagues refused to attend his ordination. While he believed that "men are able to judge what is true and right," he also believed that "those of the lower classes can go but a little way with their inquiries."[22] Because the common people were not intellectually capable of advancing very far, the world needed to rely upon those with superior knowledge and education to maintain order. This was one of the reasons that Mayhew and other liberals feared the revival—it meant shaking up the order of a society with itinerant, unqualified ministers preaching wherever the spirit moved them and then forming separatist churches. Both threatened a stable society where the clergy maintained order and control. Heimert says it was the evangelicals who embodied a more radical and democratic thrust.

Many of the liberals became Tories when the revolution occurred. This was especially true in central and western Massachusetts. Years ago as a graduate student in American history at the University of New Hampshire, I researched the history of my home town of New Salem, Massachusetts. I found that New Salem's First Parish, which gathered in 1742, became Unitarian in 1823, but had already been heading in that direction for a long time. Some of these rural churches could begin to be identified religiously by how they responded to the Great Awakening in the 1740s. Clergy who opposed the revival often became liberals, but some of their opposition to the revival was due to the nature and style of political upheaval, which threatened the social order. The difference between liberal clergy and liberal parishioners may have played a role in the downfall of certain clergy. The liberal clergy greatly valued social order and viewed themselves as an educated class apart from their parishioners. Therefore they could not condone the disruptions and criticisms of the prevailing social order that the American Revolution would cause.

Many of the Arminian clergy in Hampshire County Massachusetts were Tories who lost their pulpits during the war. In New Salem, for example, Rev. Samuel Kendall was part of this group of liberal clergy who opposed the coming revolution. When the British Governor Thomas Hutchison, a prominent loyalist, took office in 1771, these clergy members sent a letter of congratulations to him.

Dissenting religious groups were also a threat to the Standing Order clergy. The Great Awakening had started a process that heralded the coming of Baptists, Methodists, and Universalists to challenge the Congregational system. These dissenting groups were often subject to taxation and even property seizures. The Baptist minister in New Salem wrote:

> It is in my opinion that the gospel leaves it in the hands of the individuals to say how much and in what specie they shall give their teacher, and if the Church should think any of her members deficient they might stir them up to their duty . . . but not to proceed in a course of discipline against them.[23]

The liberal clergy spoke out of one side of their mouths saying they approved of the right of private judgment in matters of faith. Yet, the threat to their positions of authority in the political and social order led to countless instances of prejudicial action. Universalist preacher Nathaniel Stacy later reported that Warren Pierce, the Unitarian minister in New Salem, refused to give him a character reference to teach in Vermont, even though they had known each other since boyhood. Stacy said, "I applied in vain. . . . He meant to use his prerogative to crush me, if in his power."[24]

By contrast, the rural Arminian laity evaluated the changes in the social order and the revolution in a different manner. Like the clergy, they valued reason highly, but it was not to be confined to an intellectual elite. They wished for a public enlightenment, and this allowed them to criticize the prevailing social order. The Committee of Correspondence in New Salem wrote "We are all, even rulers themselves, and Ministers of the Gospel, subject to the same laws, as the common people."[25]

An enduring stereotype holds that Unitarianism particularly attracts wealthy and educated people. It is historically accurate that those who are more comfortable in this life tend to be less concerned about salvation and what will befall them in the next life. As Niebuhr taught, those who stand at the bottom of the social order often find a faith that assures them that they will be rewarded by God in the end and have ultimate victory. Those at the top of the social order in the Congregational system in New England were most typically the Arminians.

In the revolutionary years, more and more dissenters argued for the freedom to worship as they wished. Eventually most were given the right to form their own churches, but in certain towns, churches of various denominations were declared illegitimate by authorities and forced to battle legally for their right to exist. The Universalists in Gloucester took the Parish Church to court to win this right. What is perhaps most astounding about all this is that the liberal wing of the Congregational Church in Massachusetts—which said that faith should be ethical, non-dogmatic, and give each person the right of private judgment about their beliefs—made no effort to disestablish the state church.

Unitarian Universalists today are the children of that Parish Church that was established for the entire town to follow without exception, as well as the children of the Gloucester Universalists, who fought the establishment. Even as Unitarianism began to develop into a non-dogmatic faith that welcomed a broad spectrum of thought, its leaders continued to argue that the church should be an arm of the state that brings civic morality and religion to the whole community.

How did our Unitarian ancestors reconcile freedom of belief with this authority to impose faith? As contemporary Unitarian Universalists, do we feel a conflict between class and privilege that we are uncertain how to reconcile with our lives? Right from the beginning, Unitarians confronted the question of whether a democratic practice could match democratic theology.

The idea that Unitarians represent an elite establishment makes it easy to bash them. We can recall their privileged position in the world with Emerson's description of corpse cold liberals from Brattle Street. Emerson was concerned about class issues. He was poor as a child—especially after his father's death when he was five. Nevertheless, as an adult, he would come to view industrialization as liberating. He wrote, "We rail at trade, but the historian of the future will see that it was the principle of liberty; that it settled America, and destroyed feudalism, and made peace and keeps the peace; that it will abolish slavery." As John Patrick Diggins points out in an article on "Transcendentalism and the Spirit of Capitalism," Emerson trusted self-reliant individuals, and he believed that "wealth brings with it its own checks and balances."[26] While Marx said the competitive market will subordinate people, Emerson seemed to feel it would liberate them. Perhaps the pursuit of wealth seemed less liberating in the Gilded Age, as slums and ghettoes formed in American cities.

Class is a subject that some seem to want to avoid. When I was theme speaker on this topic at Ferry Beach for Unitarian Universalist Heritage Week in 2006, the catalog said that it was gutsy to take on the one topic Unitarian Universalists don't want to talk about. I learned this first hand when I spoke to my colleague Terry Burke. He said that a few years ago he was asked to be part of a panel that was going to speak at our district ministers' group. A couple of weeks before the scheduled event, he was told the program had been changed. Class was too hot a topic.

In some ways the question of class may ask us to move beyond our comfort zone more than gender, race, or sexual identity. This is because we perceive the people who are from another class as being so different from us in values. We have tried to bridge the three other areas of discrimination and bigotry with audits, inclusive worship, and welcoming practices. We can accept African Americans and gay people who have our same perceived liberal values, but we are reticent to embrace those we perceive as working class, uneducated, or narrow-minded. Perhaps we are too quick to dismiss the truth that all classes have folks who are smart, inquisitive people with inquiring minds and hearts open to all kinds of people. We should not sell our faith short when it comes to what we have to offer, and why we want others to join us.

While we mouth the words that our faith calls us to love the other no matter who they are, or from what class, we have never put that Universalist theology into practice. It is not easy for us to overcome our liberal sense that we know what is right for the world. We often laud Olympia Brown, the first woman anywhere to be ordained to the ministry with full denominational authority. She came from a family of Universalist farmers from Michigan. She not only ministered in the face of prejudice but also became a leader in the suffrage movement and was fired from one ministry because of her political involvement. What an inspiration to us! Yet even with all these gifts to the world, hear what she said about immigrant men who were getting the vote, a fact that was surely infuriating as she worked for women's suffrage. She wrote: "We are the first people to try the experiment of enfranchising igno-rance, drunkenness, and all forms of vice, and subordinate intel-ligence, patriotism, religion."[27] When push came to shove, Brown asserted the supremacy of the white race over blacks and immi-grants, as she predicted the enfranchisement of white women would maintain the free society of "American institutions," where "purity, temperance, and home" were preserved.[28]

In the early nineteenth century, a young woman named Lucy Barnes, the daughter of the first Universalist minister in Maine, wrote a book called *The Female Christian*. In that work she wrote that human relationships provide a model for understanding her relationship with divinity. One of her arguments for universal sal-vation was based on the emotional bonds of friendship. Sympathy, she said, ties all hearts together, and among friends it makes us feel each other's pain. As a result, she said she could not know heaven's joy while believing that millions were suffering in misery.[29]

So, too, we must ask how can we speak about an open, inclusive theology when our congregations clearly reflect that we have not been able to welcome those of other classes. Instead, our "all" is the narrow social circle of the upper-middle class, the educated few, or the like-minded liberals that we attract. This issue has plagued American liberals from the very beginning, as we emerged from a true establishment of privilege and power. Yet our British ancestors were not class-bound. Forced outside the establishment, many of them eventually achieved a certain amount of status and wealth, but some still believed that this liberal faith could appeal to a wider group of folks. Both the Americans and the British developed central beliefs in the power of education to bring personal salvation. This belief often implied that a liberal faith could be promulgated broadly. The question persists: Can we proselytize our liberal message in an intentional manner so that we become a people who not only profess a diverse and inclusive faith but also have religious communities that reflect actual diversity and thus make Unitarian Universalism more than a class-bound faith?

Brahmin Culture for the Masses

B EFORE 1740, the Congregational clergy dominated the social, cultural, religious, and even political landscape of Massachusetts. The Standing Order provided social cohesion and religious power and control. The religious revivalism of the Great Awakening loosened those fetters. Church order was torn asunder as uneducated evangelical preachers rode through the towns and disrupted religious life. The American Revolution continued that process, with rebelliousness as the zeitgeist of the times. These disruptions affected nearly every town in Massachusetts, including my home town of New Salem. There the First Parish Church became Unitarian in 1823 after nearly 100 years of existence, while withstanding the challenges of Baptists, Universalists, and Trinitarian Congregationalists.

The church had already been heading in a Unitarian direction, as it was one of those congregations that opposed the revival in the 1740s. Clergy who spoke out against the revival often became liberals, and the congregations they served reflected that. They were generally in favor of settled ministry rather than itinerancy; an educated ministry rather than one based on dramatic experiences of conversion; and an ordered society based on tax support for legitimate congregations rather than voluntary support and liberty for multiple religious sects. Yet the oldest congregation in

New Salem did not succeed. It represents the decline and failure of rural Unitarianism, a phenomenon based partly on class issues.

The failure of Unitarianism in New Salem, however, had several causes. The disestablishment of the Standing Order of Congregational churches in 1833 gave many people the impetus to leave these parishes since they were only obligated to be part of them due to the taxation system. In his doctoral dissertation, Richard Eddy Sykes refers to disestablishment as the most significant event in Unitarian history.[1] Unitarians operated under the illusion that they were leading a large church, but in fact most people were affiliated because state law required it. Once disestablishment occurred, the Unitarians realized that very few people were actually committed to the doctrines of Unitarianism.

In his *Sober Thoughts on the State of the Times*, Henry Ware Jr. expressed his fears about the Unitarians "being a community by ourselves." He called the separation of church and state "a crisis of unspeakable interest to us." He seemed panicked over what the nature and character of Unitarian institutions would be and was "oppressed with the magnitude and solemnity of the question." He went on to say that many people were attached to Unitarian churches because they disliked Calvinism, "but like nothing else . . . they are anti-Calvinists, anti-orthodox, anti-zealots, anti-everything severe and urgent in religion."[2]

Significant additional factors contributed to the failure of rural Unitarianism. Many of these communities suffered because people moved west or to the cities, looking for land ownership or employment opportunities. This was made inevitable when the railroads, industrial development, and other potential economic boons passed them by. Especially striking in New Salem, though, was the failure of Unitarianism to appeal to people whom Alpheus Harding, the minister, described as a class apart.

Harding served the New Salem congregation from 1807 to 1845 and carried on an interesting correspondence with the American Unitarian Association secretary Charles Briggs. In 1835 Harding wrote,

> My society is generally composed of the farming class and in moderate circumstances as to wealth. They have felt unable to give, and perhaps too much indisposed to read; I mean they are not a reading people. They do not feel that deep and lively interest in support of religious institutions which this importance demands [subscribing to Unitarian periodicals]. There is a coldness; they would be glad to have Unitarian views prevail and should; but enjoying their own views, they feel no disposition to urge them on others; and they would be glad to have religious institutions sustained, but they are not so ready to lend a helping hand.[3]

Waiting for the slow influence of reading periodicals to take effect did not do much for converting rural folks to liberal religion. There were class differences—rural farmers did not read much. Yet there were also some commonalities of style—the Unitarians were not evangelical in Boston, and neither were the rural Unitarians. This was that same lack of zeal that Ware noted. Since reading periodicals was not a good method of proselytizing in the country, perhaps a more pietistic approach would have gleaned more converts.

In his book *The Crisis of the Standing Order*, Peter Field says that the liberal ministers of greater Boston purposefully moved away from pietism and transformed religious expression into a secular high culture. Field argues that the disintegration of the Standing Order meant that the liberal clergy feared losing their prestigious privilege. While churches and ministers became more and more diverse, the clergy chose to become "self-serving exponents of distinct, class-based interests."

In a way the high culture became a religious substitute as it sought to refine the person and elevate the mind. This high culture was expressed through the Boston Athenaeum, the developing elitism of Harvard College, the conspicuous consumption of the merchant elite, and through publications like the *Monthly Anthology*. Field says the elitism and exclusivity curbed the spread of Unitarianism. Prominent historian Henry Adams observed a "social hierarchy" of wealth and culture. Some of the ministers affirmed this through their preaching. Joseph Stevens Buckminster of the Brattle Street Church said that the Savior does not require people "to throw their wealth into the sea or to inflict upon themselves unnatural austerities." Nothing, he continued, indicates that we should refuse the "riches, honors, and pleasures" of this world.[4]

I have suggested there was historically a class failure of rural Unitarianism. But what is striking today is the continued struggle for Unitarian Universalism to thrive in traditional working class towns, where riches and honors are fewer, and the population is not refined. In recent decades, Unitarian Universalist churches have closed in the greater Boston area towns of Stoneham, Woburn, and Lowell, and Saugus recently sold its building, essentially merging with Malden. Meanwhile, the churches in more affluent suburbs prosper. The history of Watertown, Massachusetts, where

I serve, mirrors that of some of these other towns that were once heavily industrialized. The major influx of Catholic and Orthodox immigrants from eastern or southern Europe meant that the traditional WASPs moved out.

Before these demographic changes, the economic power and cultural control of the Unitarians predominated in most of the communities of eastern Massachusetts. When Lyman Beecher was crusading for converts to his brand of evangelical Congregationalism he was appalled by the prestige and power that confronted him in Boston in 1826. In his autobiography, his daughter Harriet is quoted: "All the literary men of Massachusetts were Unitarian; all the trustees and professors of Harvard College were Unitarians; all the elite of wealth and fashion crowded Unitarian churches; the judges on the bench were Unitarian."[5]

We often talk as though all the Boston-area Unitarians were rich, snobby Brahmins, but we know there were many members who were hard working and middle class. It may be that those who enjoyed worldly success, superior educational attainments, and elite status found it difficult to reach beyond the confines of their culture. Most wealthy Unitarians did not live near or have friendships with lower or working class folk except in a paternalistic way, such as giving money or funding programs that attempted to elevate the masses to a more cultured and refined level.

The casual student of Unitarian history might say that while the Unitarians controlled all the educational, social, economic and political power in Boston, this was a good thing. The myth among us is that Unitarianism has always been liberal—not only theologically, but in literature, politics, and social action as well. This myth has been promulgated by scholars both long ago and more recently.

An article by Jane and William Pease, "Whose Right Hand of Fellowship? Pew and Pulpit in Shaping Church Practice," cites the research of Ronald Story, whose exploration of Unitarians in the nineteenth century refutes this liberal picture. He describes "middle-period" Unitarians (1850) as rich and powerful men who dominated Boston's intellectual and philanthropic organizations. These men shaped the organizations not to "melioristic liberalism but to their own exclusive, conservative, and business-oriented values." The Peases use demographic analysis to make their conclusions about nineteenth-century Boston. Of the three major sects—Episcopal, Congregational, and Unitarian—the Unitarians were most likely to enjoy political or economic power. The Unitarians represented about half of the corporate directors, a third of those with assessed property values of more than $30,000, and a third of those who held city, state, or federal office.

Significant and rapid changes in occupational patterns occurred in Unitarian parishes in the nineteenth century. The most obvious change was the decline in the number of farmers, while the merchant and manufacturing classes grew tremendously. At its earliest development, Unitarian churches included a large membership of farmers, but this changed rapidly with the economy. The Peases say that by the 1830s the Unitarians made the decisions that shaped the city's economy. Compared to other denominations, Unitarians had twenty-two times more lawyers, twenty times the number of bankers, twice as many merchants, and twenty-eight times the number of manufacturers. But they had almost no farmers, craftsmen, or industrial proletariats. By 1870 Unitarians were almost entirely upper-middle and upper class. Their economic, educational, and political success and control was remarkable. All of these realms of influence formed alliances, and nowhere was this more apparent than with Harvard College.[6]

Just as Charles Chauncy had depicted heaven as a glorified Harvard Graduate School for the majority of Unitarians, Harvard was what guaranteed heavenly success on earth in whatever career choice you made. This is the thesis of *Harvard and the Boston Upper Class: The Forging of an Aristocracy, 1800–1870* by Ronald Story. Before the mid-nineteenth century, prominent Boston Unitarians were frequently called *elite*, but this changed just after the Civil War, when they were more commonly referred to as *upper class*. By 1870 the rich and the well-born, as well as the culturally cultivated, were referred to as *Brahmins*. This development included several key elements. First, one accumulated wealth, especially through entrepreneurship. One merchant said, "A man without money is like a body without a soul."[7] This entrepreneurial wealth was combined and consolidated through the second key component: kinship. The Boston Brahmins were a group that depended upon class intermarriage, such as cousins with cousins or only Lowells and Cabots talking to each other. Third, one protected this class structure through politics.

The role of culture in the formation of the Brahmin elite is extremely important. Georgiana Bruce Kirby was an immigrant from England who first worked as a nursemaid for Rev. Ezra Stiles Gannett and his wife Anna Tilden. Kirby recorded some of her responses to Brahmin Boston in her journal, published as *Georgi-*

ana: Feminist Reformer of the West. She found that the class distinctions in Boston were more severe than those she experienced at home. She wrote,

> It did not take long for me to learn that the caste spirit in Boston was harder, more insensitive than in the mother-country. Its basis was not inherited estates and titles, but descent either from those Puritans who came over in the May-flower, or from other early emigrants of that class.

You needed to belong to certain families. Georgiana resented the "petty assumption" of her employers, but she endured "the furnace of Boston conservatism" for more than three years. During this time she read all the Unitarian literature and converted.[8]

Religion was a factor in developing a culturally coherent elite. In 1850 two-thirds of the wealthiest Bostonians were Unitarians. By 1870, the average Unitarian was thirteen times richer than the average member of any other denomination. Unitarian beliefs offered fewer constraints on worldly success. The Unitarians were responsible for the establishment of a number of cultural institutions, but they often kept them private. The Boston Athenaeum, for instance, was controlled by proprietors who opposed its public use. They did not want to throw open its doors to the "many-headed" rabble. Following the example of England, they wanted to make everyone pay.

Thoreau wrote that the Lowell Institute, an educational foundation that was suppose to provide free public lectures, excluded the "ignorant and critical classes of society," and "the lean, hungry, savage, anti-everythings." In addition to being exclusive, Thoreau found the lectures to be "as tame as the settled ministers," thereby indicating a fear of saying anything too political or controversial.[9]

Thus the institutions were linked in a classist power structure independent of popular control. Historian Anne Rose discusses the defensive self-containment of the upper classes, noting that those who stepped beyond permissible boundaries could be excluded. After Lydia Maria Child published her book *An Appeal in Favor of that Class of Americans Called Africans*, the Athenaeum revoked her reading privileges. Child saw it as her duty to defend the liberty of the slaves, but as Rose notes, "liberty became license when it threatened prosperity and order." Bronson Alcott later lost his reading privileges, too. Some Athenaeum members questioned the publication of William Ellery Channing's book *Slavery*, thinking it might disturb the internal, domestic relations in the slave-holding states. Rose says the culture became increasingly insular as the number of immigrants increased.

After 1830 wealth was concentrated in the same few hands, and it was difficult to enter the groups of those who had incomes over $10,000. From 1830 to 1860, this group simply became older without adding new younger members. The elite deliberately closed its ranks.[10] The period after 1830 also witnessed the formation of the first labor unions. Many of these organizations advocated free public education, the end of monopolies, and the abolition of imprisonment for debt. They began to exert their rights and liberties as American citizens, and while Unitarians advocated these values in their religious system, they became anxious when democracy and equality were applied to local political and economic issues.

The expansion of Harvard College best exemplifies this growth of private institutions. It depended at first upon a small group of private donors and was not publicly funded. Of twenty-eight large-scale donors before 1850, all but two were Unitarians. University expansion was built upon wealthy, enterprising, politically conservative but theologically liberal families. From 1805 to 1860, thirty-six members were elected to the Harvard Corporation. Thirty-three were Unitarian. Eighty percent of the faculty were also Unitarian. The faculty were also conservative on social and political issues.

Not happy with the pantheism and innate human divinity in Transcendentalism, Harvard's most famous scientist, Louis Aggasiz, believed in a development theory of nature which produced a social hierarchy that supported racial supremacy. He followed a non-scriptural, deistic system which conformed to the framework of the institution's elite sponsors. He was against programs to uplift the poor and blacks, whom his science proclaimed inferior.

The Harvard student body was elitist, too. By the mid 1850s the student body was three-quarters Unitarian. Elite progeny commonly chose to matriculate there, but a poor person could not afford it. It was the seminary and academy for the inner circle of Bostonians. Theodore Parker wrote,

The poor man's son, however well-born, struggling for a superior education, obtains his culture at a monstrous cost; with the sacrifice of pleasure, comfort, the joys of youth, often of eyesight and health. . . . The rich man's son needs not that terrible trial. He learns from his circumstances, not his soul. . . . All the outward means of educating, refining, elevating a child, are to be had for money, and money alone.[11]

Harvard students trained to achieve a class status that would keep them from mixing with the rabble. Harvard established its own church after Cambridge acquired its first lower class congregations, including Universalist. The church leaders strived for gentlemanly qualities. There are regular references against the vulgar, the tawdry, the disorderly, and undesirables. These discriminatory tactics were aimed at rural elements at first, and later immigrants, who were described as "drunken," "unkempt," and "vicious."

Some evidence indicates that Unitarian congregations opposed reform activism. Historian Richard Eddy Sykes quotes Rev. Francis LeBaron, a minister in Worcester who was concerned that the Unitarians were neglecting the poor: "I do wish that men of capital and influence would turn their attention to the dwellings of the poor in this city while there is yet time before numbers make it almost a hopeless task."[12]

Jane and William Pease also see this opposition in the infamous case of John Pierpont at the Hollis Street Church in Boston. Pierpont asked his congregation to confront issues of abolition and temperance. In 1838 Pierpont became an advocate for proposed legislation which would restrict sales of liquor except to those who bought in very large quantities. He was an activist on the issue, and his public role turned some of his parishioners against him. In a congregational report, the proprietors of the church accused him of a variety of failings including poor pastoral relations, dabbling in phrenology, and of "entering into every exciting topic" in sermons, as Pierpont later reported in *Proceedings of a Meeting of Friends of Rev. John Pierpont and his Reply to the Charges of the Committee of Hollis Street Society*. He refuted the charges, but distillers and merchants in the trade continued the attack, buying up enough vacant pews to eventually force him to resign his pastorate. It took them until 1845, by which date they were withholding salary.[13]

The Peases cite conflicting values in these battles between the reform-minded and the defenders of the business ethic. Nathan Appleton, a member of Boston's Federal Street Church and the owner of a cotton mill in Waltham, Massachusetts, wrote that there "was no purer morality than that of the counting house." The central belief in individual freedom of faith included the right of "every individual . . . to the benefit of his own acquisitions." Finally, the Peases quote David Robinson in the context of commenting on the implications of all Unitarian social activism: "It was rarely if ever a threat to the established economic order in America." The Peases note that we must consider the implications of this unwillingness to question the capitalist nature of the economy for the classes that would be included within the Unitarian fold.[14]

The Unitarians were not entirely class-bound. Some individuals embraced a different vision of society than those who were so economically and socially successful. One such person was Bernard Whitman. Whitman was a Unitarian minister who worked to spread Unitarianism beyond New England and the educated class. One of thirteen children and a native of East Bridgewater, Massachusetts, he had to interrupt his studies frequently to earn money. As a student he was suspended from Harvard for defending his roommate, who was involved in a mock battle between the freshmen and sophomores in the commons. He studied with more than one mentor and then in 1825 was called to the new Second Religious Society in Waltham, Massachusetts—a church gathered a few years earlier for the workers and managers of the recently founded textile mills.

Women who were recruited to work in the mills were among his parishioners. Their care and education became one of the responsibilities of the area churches. Whitman also had prior experience in organizing ladies social circles. In 1827 he noticed his wood pile was disappearing too rapidly, and he decided to keep a watch on it. One night he noticed a woman whom he recognized as one of his parishioners carrying away an armful of wood. He said nothing but investigated and discovered she was destitute. Calling together the women of the parish, he suggested they help her with gifts of clothes and other necessities. This was the beginning of the Female Charitable Society. He also gave lectures on grammar and geography to female factory workers and organized young men into what became the lyceum, the Rumford Institute. This later led to the formation of the first free public library in Waltham. He was minister there from 1826 until 1834, when he died.[15]

Whitman did not like being identified as a Unitarian. He opposed both sectarian names and any statement of belief, like many Unitarians of his time. Theologically, doctrines were secondary to him. He was more concerned with the formation of Christian character and the promotion of practical religion. He wanted to extend Unitarianism that it might be less sectarian and more clearly a part of the church universal. He traveled all over to preach the faith, including evangelical missions to Kentucky and Ohio. Unitarianism was not only for the wealthy and learned classes but was truth for all. In his biography of Whitman in the online "Dictionary of Unitarian Universalist Biography," Peter Hughes writes, "His preaching appealed to laborers in the mills who wished to hear his plain and practical sermons."

Whitman encouraged young men to enter the ministry, even if they could not afford an education. "I admit the more learning the better," he said, but he also believed that Unitarian extension demanded more variety in the ministry. Less-learned ministers were often "the best men for many places because plain in their manner of preaching, ardent, [they] have entered upon the work from their interest in the success of religion and not because they have got through college and must have a profession." Whitman also associated broadly with restorationist Universalists, those who believed in some period of punishment after death.

In 1832 he preached at the installation service in Mendon, Massachusetts, for Adin Ballou, the great Universalist preacher and founder of the Hopedale Community. In that address Whitman called for a broad-based Christian faith, as was reflected in his title, "Christian Union." His formula for the pure faith was:

- no sectarian names, just Christian
- no creeds, only the scriptures as a standard of faith
- religious liberty
- no church hierarchy
- ministers should teach people how to live, not what to believe
- all obey the golden rule.

Whitman's was a lonely voice for calling for a broader-based Unitarianism.[16]

Despite Whitman's interest in promulgating a message attractive to working people, he has also been characterized as an apologist for industrialization. In his dissertation on *Massachusetts Unitarianism and Social Change*, Richard Eddy Sykes notes that Whitman believed that American factory workers received higher wages than workers in England and extreme poverty did not exist. Sykes adds that Whitman said he had been associated with five factories and that none practiced corporal punishment. The proprietors provided for the education of their workers, offering lectures and access to libraries. Whitman also said that in America, workers could improve themselves. He believed that success could be achieved through hard work, and he emphasized self-discipline and self-improvement. The economic system was a good one, offering all the opportunity for advancement.

Sykes goes on to say that a great many Unitarians claimed that labor and management had the same interests. Amos Lawrence, a cotton factory owner and philanthropist, wrote, "We are all workingmen; and the attempt to get up a Working-man's party is a libel upon the whole population, as it implies that there are among us large numbers who are not working-men." The burden of their pleas, Sykes says, "always ended in an apology for the existing class structure."[17] Some of this feeling emanated from an early optimism about the possibilities for America to be fair and good, but by the late 1840s urban problems resulting from industrialization were becoming more and more severe.

Whitman may also represent conflicting values within Unitarianism. The faith was grounded in the potential of the individual to achieve success, and in the goodness in the heart of each person. While Whitman may have wanted a broader-based Unitarian faith, his values prevented him from understanding the terrible deprivations that might result from the accumulation of power and wealth.

Samuel Longfellow, Henry's brother, noticed this when he was called to the church in Fall River. While candidating he found that the people were absorbed with money-making. Once settled, he noticed little advocacy for the poor, and in one sermon he begged his parishioners to show some concern and apply their Christian values to the deplorable conditions in the city. Longfellow observed that Christianity and capitalism were based upon different values. The accumulation of wealth was founded upon "organizing competition and antagonism instead of cooperation and brotherhood."[18]

Octavius Brooks Frothingham, a Transcendentalist whose father had been minister of the First Church of Boston, characterized the Unitarians as "conservative, believers in providential arrangements of society, believers in respectability, in class distinctions." There was to be no "sudden overturning or any *overturning* at all" of the social order. "Their faith was in slow and gradual uplifting, through the diffusion of charity and the spread of faith."[19]

The mantle of trying to achieve a broader-based Unitarianism passed in the next generation from Bernard Whitman to Arthur Buckminster Fuller, Margaret Fuller's younger brother and a one-time minister in Watertown, Massachusetts. In his biography of Arthur Fuller, Joseph Herring says that Arthur "endeavored to give the Unitarian church appeal to all social classes and championed the important social reforms of the day." Fuller's father died when he was thirteen. He worked the family farm, and his sister Margaret helped raise him and ensured that he received a proper education in preparation for college. With limited financial resources, Arthur had to devote some of his time while at Harvard to teaching in local schools to support himself. Before he attended divinity school, he went west and became a lay missionary, preaching over a wide area in Illinois. After graduating from Harvard Divinity School, he served a congregation in Manchester, New Hampshire, for five years. Later he served at the New North Church in Boston, where "Mother" Taylor, wife of the famous Methodist preacher Father Taylor of Boston's Seaman's Chapel, heard him speak. Apparently his evangelical style helped convince her that "others are going to heaven besides Methodists." Fuller believed in extemporaneous preaching, which was at odds with the more typical manuscript lecture style of his colleagues.[20]

The New North Church was situated in a changing neighborhood, eventually dominated by immigrant Italian Catholics. Fuller characterized expanding the congregation as a Sisyphean task, but he did the best he could rather than abandon the neighborhood. Shunning denominationalism, he was a force behind the church having no sectarian name, preferring to aspire to a "oneness of the followers of Christ." He emphasized the growth of the Sabbath School, where destitute children were taken in. His Baptist colleague in Boston said that Fuller was a "friend of the poor and the outcast." Herring writes that Fuller believed that workers, farmers, and other "common folk would flock to Unitarianism if they received the word of God in their own simple language."

Fuller was an advocate of many of the reforms of his day, including temperance, abolitionism, and public education. In his temperance work it was said he was "bringing men of different callings and religious persuasions into friendly nearness."[21] In

1859 he was called to serve the church in Watertown, but when the war broke out, he resigned and became a regimental chaplain. Just after Lincoln took office, Fuller spoke at a public meeting in Watertown, where he protested any further compromise with slavery. He said, "Let us stand right ourselves, and then we can demand right from others."[22]

During a leave from his duties he received a gift of $250 from his colleagues in Watertown, with participation from every denomination, including the Catholic priest. He was honorably discharged on December 10, 1862, as he was not medically fit for duty. The very next day he volunteered to help serve on the boats that were to ferry troops across the Rappahannock River. He joined the 19th Massachusetts regiment on the other side, and he took a place along the skirmish line as troops assaulted Fredericksburg. He was killed within minutes.

A more inclusive vision for Unitarianism was also seen in the work of some of the Romantic era writers, including Margaret Fuller and Herman Melville. Ann Douglas, in her book *The Feminization of American Culture*, hailed these two as class heroes many years ago. After Fuller went to work for Horace Greeley, she wrote pieces for the *New York Tribune* on slavery, prisons, and labor. She became increasingly aware that American preeminence in the world was based on abusing various classes of people—blacks, immigrants, Indians, and, above all, women.

She discovered subtler forms of oppression than merely economic exploitation. The culture degraded Indians and destroyed their self-respect. The same thing happened to women. She fought myths that Indians were lazy and women intellectually incapable.[23] Fuller, her brother, and Bernard Whitman all felt limited or

constrained in the pursuit of their careers by economic consider-
ations. As it was for Theodore Parker, money was an issue for
them, and their private struggles helped them relate personally
to economic injustices in the world. They also pushed social conventions. Fuller even went to the extreme of participating in a
revolution in Italy.

Melville wrote of the power of social structures rather than
individual personality as a determining factor in our lives in many
of his works, including *Moby Dick* and *Billy Budd*. His books
describe confrontations between employer and employee or captain and sailor. This was an important counterpoint to the highly
personal Unitarian faith, where one achieves fulfillment through
self-improvement. Melville writes that there is a power beyond
the personal that oppresses. He also emphasizes the lost or forgot-
ten. No one talks of class difference in the culture, he believed,
because it is ignored. He tried to rectify this by writing of common
sailors, immigrants, blacks, and city clerks.[24]

Yet Melville's common folk did not feel an easy welcome when
they attended Unitarian churches. In 1846 a letter was sent to the
Christian Register about a person who tried to visit a church where
a renowned minister held forth. The visitor stood outside for a
time and finally asked if there was any provision for strangers. The
person he asked said, "We are rather exclusive here," and then
went into the church without offering assistance. The tradition of
not speaking to visitors has a mythic foundation in our history.
Even if visitors walked through the doors, they probably found
no place to sit as most of the pews were already restricted to people
who owned them. Visitors could take second-class seating in the
balcony, where congregations traditionally seated slaves.[25]

The lack of place for the poor in Unitarian congregations in Boston was underscored by the work of Joseph Tuckerman. His ministry to the poor began as the Ministry at Large in 1826 and continues to this day as the Unitarian Universalist Urban Ministry. Tuckerman wrote that only the pew proprietors were welcomed at worship; the poor "cannot pay for the privilege, in the largest number of our places of worship have at best a very narrow space appropriated for them, and there they must sit apart, as 'the class of the poor.' " He noted how this was inconsistent with the principles of Christianity, and that the poor were made to feel like a "caste."[26]

Tuckerman began to see his role as a parish minister in the context of the entire community when he was settled in Chelsea, Massachusetts. Despite having an orientation that equated poverty with crime and sinfulness, Tuckerman saw his mission to elevate the masses as to "enable every individual to surmount every obstacle in the way to the highest moral completeness within his attainment." Thus the "drain digger" and the "scavenger" could be as morally complete as the most exalted.[27] Tuckerman wanted the more favored classes to understand the realities of poverty, but only wished to support the poor through voluntary charity. He feared that public support would institutionalize pauperism. Nevertheless, he wanted to create moral connections between rich and poor. He said the rich should have "a knowledge of poverty and of the poor, which is not otherwise to be obtained."[28] Tuckerman was disturbed by class distinctions and believed that relationships between the classes would alleviate some of the distance.

Within a year of its founding, Tuckerman's Ministry had constructed its first chapel at Friend Street. Other ministers replicated

Tuckerman's visitation to people's homes, and soon more than a hundred volunteers were helping instruct children and adults alike in such skills as reading and sewing. Although Tuckerman was concerned that separate congregations for the poor would reinforce the class structure, the chapels created by the Ministry at Large became important community centers for the poor of Boston.

Others became concerned about class in even more revolutionary ways than mere cordial relationships between the classes. George Ripley, who gained fame as the founder of the utopian community at Brook Farm, married into a wealthy family, but his views of the world were influenced by the writing and example of Orestes Brownson, a radical who would make the journey from Universalism to Unitarianism to Catholicism. Brownson compared wage labor to slavery and rejected William Ellery Channing's view that advocated the need for the working classes to seek personal moral improvement. Instead he advocated listening to labor's demands for economic justice.

The Unitarians tended to sacrifice social justice to their need for harmony, and the idea of one class agitating for power was dangerous to them. Brownson seemed to understand class struggle more than his Unitarian colleagues, and while they listened to him, he did not experience much acceptance among them. Channing was disturbed by Brownson's "The Laboring Classes" and told Elizabeth Palmer Peabody that Brownson had exaggerated the hardships of working class people. They were better off than lawyers and merchants, Channing said, because they did not aspire as high and therefore would be less liable to disappointment when they failed. Channing wrote, "No good can come but from the spread of intellectual and moral power among all classes." Brownson felt that Channing was cool toward him because he "was not brought up among us."[29]

Brownson eventually converted to Catholicism. But most Unitarian clergy saw that religion as a superstitious, authoritarian, foreign faith practiced by poor, unwashed immigrants, whose poverty was directly related to their lack of a frugal, disciplined, and individualistic Protestant work ethic. The ethic of Unitarianism was that of the self-made man. The new self-help literature dealt not with business or accounting but with the development of character, and Unitarian clergy were among the most prominent self-help writers. Channing used the term *self-culture* to reinforce the ideal that the individual could be successful if he/she develops the habits of hard work, frugality, perseverance, and sobriety. The Unitarians wanted to elevate the masses morally to their level and believed that those who would pit classes against one another threatened the stability of society.[30]

Many of the poorer, immigrant populations suffered from a multitude of problems. George Ripley was among the first to notice this after he was called as minister to the Purchase Street Church in Boston in 1826. This small congregation of the "middling classes" was located near one of the wharves. Ripley's ministry had gone well, but after the Panic of 1837, an economic crisis that brought high unemployment, he became more and more concerned about the laboring classes, especially in his own neighborhood. In his sermon, "The Temptations of the Times," he expressed dismay over the inordinate pursuit and worship of wealth founded upon "temptations to an excess of selfishness."[31]

Ripley wanted to serve the poor but didn't quite know how to respond to his new mission. Finally, he became convinced that parish ministry was too economically entangled with making comfortable and smug parishioners happy while others suffered from poverty and hunger and had few educational opportunities. In his "Letter of Intent to Resign," he indicated how he must be true to himself and that he sometimes avoided preaching on certain subjects for fear of their response. He finally said that his faith called him to establish the kingdom of God "in the living present . . . not in the dead past."[32] He also believed that faith could not simply be the improvement of personal character, but that individuals suffered from "public sin" and needed to directly confront the "evils of society." Ripley's biographer, Charles Crowe, describes Ripley's farewell sermon to his congregation as a warning that what they needed "was a revolution in commercial, political, and domestic relations rather than a mild chat on Sunday mornings."[33]

He soon became entranced with the idea of starting an entire community devoted to his ideas of social transformation. With the birth of Brook Farm in 1841, Ripley and his wife Sophia instituted a vision to balance labor and intellect so that people of all stations could be educated to "prepare a society of liberal, intelligent, and cultivated persons, whose relations with each other would permit a more simple and wholesome life than can be led amidst the pressure of our competitive institutions."[34] While Brook Farm eventually failed after adopting Charles Fourier's brand of socialism, the farm placed a major emphasis on identifying with "all classes."

At a convention in New York in 1844, Charles Dana, a journalist and the manager of the Brook Farm publication *The Harbinger*, summarized many of the successes achieved by the residents of Brook Farm. Dana noted the abolishment of domestic servitude, the education of all, and justice to the laborer, thus ennobling industry. Dana wanted to be clear in his report that this was no pipe dream, but that he was describing the actual community. All the business of life at Brook Farm was carried out without any domestics. Ripley had wanted to change people's attitudes toward labor from the beginning, so they could say that they were servants of each other and that no single person was "master." Dana said that the person who "digs a ditch or discharges any other repulsive duty is not at the foot of the social scale—he is at the head of it."[35] Similarly, Nathaniel Hawthorne once referred to the manure he shoveled at Brook Farm as the "gold."

Dana also described how education was given to all those who desired it. The community philosophy was that education was a human birthright, and not only for the wealthy and privileged. Finally, he stated that laborers received their just reward. He reported that generally economic gain fills the pocket of the employer, but at Brook Farm the results of their labors were distributed in a just fashion. How much people actually worked equaled how much they would get. This makes it easy to see why they adopted socialism. The goal was a complete reorganization of social arrangements in society. This led to many attacks upon the Brook Farm adherents by the press. They were accused of fomenting class conflict, among other immoralities. But Ripley said they were only recognizing class conflict created by capitalist exploitation that already existed. "The rude unwashed plebeians" were made to feel inferior "in education, in knowledge, in manners, in dress, in social position, but they do not perceive that the distinction is founded in justice or reason; they feel that they have been defrauded of . . . their rights."[36]

The socialists at Brook Farm reflect a fundamental conflict over saving the world. Ripley asked how clergy can truly rebuke the sins of the world and be change agents in society rather than harmless lecturers. Among the Transcendentalists, he rebuked those who affirmed the reform of self over the reform of society.

In his recent history of the Transcendentalists, Philip Gura defines this as the central conflict within the movement. Perhaps this fundamental issue has made Unitarian Universalists feel conflicted throughout their history. The promotion of individual transformation means that, while there may be individual efforts at reform, there is no vision for a communitarian transformation of society. Ripley saw his colleagues as fundamentally conservative, as preservers of the order of things, complacently at ease with the status quo.

Ripley's ministry and the Brook Farm experience raise some fundamental questions. How can the church effectively address larger issues of economic injustice that go beyond the liberation of individuals—so that larger oppressions, including ruthless business practices, can be eliminated or transformed? Can the church ever be a change agent? What can we learn from those who saw the focus of their faith in more communal, just, and relational ways with all classes?

Unitarianism was not merely the Boston religion of individual success—some had a vision of denominational and societal transformation.

Universalism and a Classless Heaven

EVEN THOUGH I did not grow up in a Universalist church, I am proud to claim Universalist roots. My mother's family were Universalists from Orange, Massachusetts. Looking through some old records I once discovered that my great uncle Ralph Verney had attended a General Assembly meeting in Florida. My parents disagreed over where their four children would be raised. While my siblings were all baptized at my father's Congregational Church, I was dedicated at the First Universalist Church in Orange by Rev. Fred Harrison. That I have become a minister makes it proof positive that Universalist determinism exists.

Today many Unitarian Universalists say they want to embrace the spiritual heritage of Universalism, thinking it was a religion of the heart rather than the head. They believe that the old Universalists wanted to experience the love of God directly and that the entire human family would be drawn up into this love. We often depict these Universalist forebears as country folk who protested an urbane intellectualism, church formalism, and comfortable social positions. There is some truth there, even outside of the New England origins. In his essay "Cousins Twice Removed: Unitarians and Universalists in the South," Charles Howe says that prior to consolidation, "the cultural and theological gulf between the two denominations remained wide. Urban, humanistic

Unitarians and small town, Christian Universalists seemed to have little common ground on which to meet."[1]

Many Universalists from the geographic area I call home were uneducated rock farmers, whom I have elsewhere called "hill country heretics."[2] These communities close to Orange include the towns of Warwick, Massachusetts, the home of Caleb Rich, and Richmond, New Hampshire, the birthplace of Hosea Ballou. These Universalist founders fit our stereotype of people who stressed direct experiences of faith through the heart and not the head. They contrasted in many ways with the elite, formal power brokers who occupied the pews of the Congregational and, later, Unitarian churches. They were drawn from a different class of people. Many were converts from the Baptist faith who were farmers and smaller property holders. In these rural areas they had often migrated from somewhere else in New England, moving en masse as families. Politically, they usually had Democratic Republican affiliations. They were Jeffersonians, while their Unitarian counterparts, like John Adams, were Federalists.

What is perhaps most startling about these early Universalists, in addition to their evangelical approach, is the understanding that the embrace of God is meant for all humanity. This contrasts sharply with the cultural underpinnings that associate salvation with individual achievement and success. Early Universalism emphasized that there was a moral community of all people in the Godhead. Central to the Universalist gospel is an egalitarian, classless idea of salvation. It is not our individual acts that will save us but our connection with that larger moral force which unites the universe. This chapter examines that classless approach, contrasts it with Unitarianism, and concludes that this class mixture was common among the Universalist faithful.[3]

In his book *The Pro and Con of Universalism*, George Rogers, who traveled thousands of miles as an itinerant Universalist preacher in the 1820s and 1830s, described his experiences at Universalist gatherings. Once, between worship services, the congregation gathered at a schoolhouse where provisions were

> spread out on a common table, to which, without respect to rank, or condition, or opinions all that would come might come, and partake freely, without money and without price. . . . All were on a parity, all distinctions of caste were lost sight of; all individualities were merged in the mass; and as one family all rejoiced together in a common and glorious hope.[4]

We may wonder if the Universalist theology of radical equality translated into an equitable mix of economic, educational, and political variations that were reflected in the parish rolls. There is some evidence that as a group Universalists were an aspiring middle class who occupied positions in all ranks and stations of life. The initial converts to Universalism were largely drawn from Baptist ranks. Liberal, educated Congregationalists were generally not attracted to the more evangelical approach of the early Universalists.

In his book *New England Dissent, 1630–1833: The Baptists and the Separation of Church and State*, William McLoughlin tells us that the records of the New England Baptist churches indicate clearly "the great inroads which the Universalists made into their membership ranks."[5] He says almost every Baptist church lost members to the Universalists. Some lost as many as ten or twenty, including seven Baptist elders who became apostates.

When John Murray first began preaching Universalism in America, many of his converts could not distinguish between his preaching and that of the great revivalist George Whitefield. Many of the fledgling Universalists were New Lights, or those who had an especially vivid experience of saving grace. Charles Chauncy, one of the leaders of the Standing Order clergy, also came to believe in universal salvation, but he was hesitant about publicly admitting it, publishing his views anonymously. He referred to Murray and the other Universalist preachers as "illiterate."[6]

Isaac Backus, the leader of the Baptists, took some solace in the popularity of the heretical doctrine among his followers because he believed it played a key role in weakening the Standing Order. Before the Newton and Watertown Universalist Church was founded in Massachusetts, Elhanan Winchester converted some of his family members and neighbors to Universalism. This defection caused an uproar in the Newton Baptist Church and eventually fifteen people were excommunicated, including two clerks. The Universalist Church in Red Hill, North Carolina, was founded in 1834, when Luther Rice converted from Baptist to Universalist and brought most of the congregation with him into the new fold.[7]

Little demographic analysis of early Universalist membership exists. In his work on *Radical Sects of Revolutionary New England*, Stephen Marini indicates that Universalists came from all walks of economic life. In Langdon, New Hampshire, Universalists owned slightly above average amounts of property and claimed members who were prominent citizens both economically and politically.

While two of their members were among the wealthiest people in town, they could claim some of the poorest people as well. This was in a marginal economy, but the distribution seems to have been a normal representation in various economic rankings.[8]

Even in a small sampling I compiled for New Salem, Massachusetts, Universalists occupied the middle ground economically. They were not the poorest group in town, which was reserved for the Baptists, but neither were they the wealthiest group either, a crown worn by the Congregationalists, who were on their way to splitting into Unitarian and Trinitarian factions. An 1811 list of polls and estates for New Salem shows that many of the known Universalists were former Congregationalists, unlike the usual pattern of attracting more evangelical types from Baptist groups. In New Salem, all the Universalists in the sample owned property, but their holdings were concentrated in the middle of the list, with none of them being especially wealthy. The mean number of acres of land owned was ninety-six, while the mean for the Congregationalists was 187.5. Ten out of the twelve largest landholders were Congregationalists.[9]

Marini says the Universalists and the other sectarian groups he studied (Shakers and Freewill Baptists) were not socially, economically, or politically deviant, but their constituencies had normal variations and were representative of the diversity in their communities. They responded as extended families to new religious ideas transmitted by charismatic leaders in evangelical style. This method of converting family groups by prophetic evangelical preaching represented a distinct difference between the Universalists and those liberal Congregationalists who came to be called Unitarians.[10]

Orestes Brownson, who traveled from Universalism to Unitarianism to Roman Catholicism, once observed that a certain "Universalist minister was a tall, majestic person, of grave and venerable aspect, a chaste and dignified speaker, and the best sermonizer I ever knew among Universalists. But he had too refined and cultivated a taste to be a popular Universalist preacher, and finally, I believe, followed my example, and associated with the Unitarians."[11]

This passage about Edward Turner may have been Brownson's method of seeking revenge against his former co-religionists, as Turner, like Brownson, rejected the more heretical aspects of Universalist theology. Yet this descriptive difference associated with class disparities of style appears with some regularity when comparing Unitarians and Universalists.

In his history of Universalism and spiritualism, John Buescher quotes from the spiritualist publication *The Religio-Philosophical Journal*, which characterizes Unitarians as holding their views in "reserve with a polite timidity which might as well be called moral cowardice." The journal editor John Curtis Bundy writes that even those ministers who held spiritualist views would not express them because one did not say such things in "polite society." Unitarians were better able to avoid confronting fellow church members, Buescher says, about direct claims concerning the reality of spirits.[12] This is an example of the Unitarian proclivity for tolerance and understanding, leaving them with the inability to express strong views that might cause conflict. They were so polite, the issues were avoided.

This matter of style affected conflicting views on an educated clergy. Universalists were sometimes accused of being too loose on their requirements for ministry. One critic said a Universalist minister's principal qualifications were an "unfurnished head, a voluble tongue, and a cockerel smartness." The ministers had zeal, he said, but some religious novelty would lead them to begin to agitate in a new direction. The Universalist leader Hosea Ballou said that the true word of Christ must be imprinted on your heart and not learned through a book. In his sermon "Feast of Knowledge," given in Pennsylvania and printed in 1832, Ballou told how to distinguish between a minister of the Lord and a minister of this world: "The minister of this world's wisdom, has not the cause of God nor our Redeemer to promote."[13]

His concern that an overly educated minister would lose his gospel faith led Ballou to oppose the establishment of Tufts College, and indeed it did not see the light of day until the year Ballou died, 1852. He did not oppose education, but theological school raised his ire. He thought this kind of training allowed clergy to "evade the plain testimony of Jesus." When the debate over the establishment of Tufts was being kindled, Ballou wrote about how the denomination first succeeded under the ministrations of unlettered preachers. He also worried that a standard academic training would stamp its graduates with one formal style, like a cookie cutter, and he preferred they experience unadulterated Christianity. The rise of Transcendentalist thinking raised further concerns that plain Bible truths must live in the hearts of people uncorrupted by the German philosophies. He wanted to appeal directly to the people in informal, homespun, and emotional ways. This style is what historian E. Brooks Holifield refers to as *populist theology*—meant to appeal to all the common people rather than the academics. Of course, such preaching represented a serious threat to the establishment.[14]

The Unitarians and the Universalists differed in style, education, and economic standing. David Bumbaugh, in his paper on class in Unitarian Universalism, tells us that it is a myth that Universalism was a lower-class faith. Despite the movement's rural, Baptist origins in the hill country, the Universalists in Gloucester organized a church with ship captains and merchants among its members. Yet the former slave Gloster Dalton was among its original members, too. Perhaps there is reason to believe that Universalism drew from all ranks of society and emerged in many kinds of places. While we know of its origins in rural places in New England, it was a town phenomenon as well. Eventually Murray moved to Boston, and Elhanan Winchester's conversion from the Baptist faith to the Universalist in Philadelphia gave Universalism its first vital urban center.

Anne Bressler, author of *The Universalist Movement in America, 1770–1870*, says that Universalism played an important role in the formation of Philadelphia's working class. Universalists "spoke of a community of love in ways that echoed the solidarity of tight-knit jouneymen's societies and the mutuality of the larger working class community." William Heighton, a shoemaker who became the leader of the Mechanic's Union of Trade Association and the Workingman's Party was a Universalist who organized many meetings in Universalist churches. Heighton led the city's labor movement for about five years around 1830. He was a working class radical who called the privileged elite parasites that must be overthrown, or the future for the workers would be a "gloomy one of endless toil and helpless poverty." The artisans he represented dominated the First Universalist Church, which had been founded by Elhanan Winchester in 1781. Many of the parishioners were trade union leaders and members of the Pennsylvania Democratic society.[15]

Heighton said Universalist preachers taught the "necessity of undeviating justice" between people. So from rural Vermont to urban centers like New York, the Universalist gospel of equality and possibility appealed to all types in all kinds of environments. This Universalist diversity ranged from the evangelical preachers in remote villages to the urban poor in the mill towns of New Hampshire. David Bumbaugh says these Universalists, whatever their station and wherever they came from, longed for respectability and some degree of educational and economic success. Many were able to achieve this as a kind of rising middle class, although they never attained the elite status of their Unitarian brothers and sisters. They were lesser merchants and shopkeepers as opposed to inherited gentility.[16]

Historian Peter Hughes characterizes the members of the First Universalist Church of Woonsocket, Rhode Island, as children of the textile mills, which once dominated the economic and social landscape of Woonsocket. Many of these Universalists had worked in the mills, and Hughes maintains that they were "blue collar to the core." They were not ordinary proletarians, however. Hughes writes,

> Unlike the tens of thousands of mill-hands who made up the greater part of the city, who were content, or at least resigned, to their status, Woonsocket Universalists never doubted that they had, or soon would, transcend their working-class or agricultural origins. These Universalists were ambitious and worked with a purpose in mind. They moved up the ladder.

Many rose to be shop stewards and foremen. Some came to own businesses of their own, such as a lumberyard or a funeral home, or else made the transition into executive positions in manufacturing or banking. Successful as they might have been, they did not pretend to be educated or leisured; they were intelligent, proud, working folk.[17]

This family background is also characteristic of the life of the Universalist minister Charles Vickery, the subject of a 1990 lecture by Carl Seaburg. Vickery came from Pittsfield, Maine, a mill town, where his father owned an insurance business. Later in his career Vickery ministered in Mexico City. When he arrived there the congregation was nothing more than a discussion group for Americans living in Mexico. He wanted to expand the congregation to include the native population as well. He worked hard to establish the relationships between the two groups, fulfilling his first conviction: "Unitarian Universalism should be available to all people." The prospective membership form for the congregation said the group had a dream of a human family "undivided by nationality, race or color." His hope was not "workers of the world unite," but "people of the world unite."[18]

Hughes tells us that one of the defining features of Universalists is their class status. People who emerged from many different classes, lower as well as upper, but more firmly rooted in a hard-working middle class, largely created Universalism. Unitarians tended to range from the middle class to the upper and educated classes. Hughes writes,

It is not that Universalists were never learned or rich. They often became so. While an intelligent Unitarian went to Harvard or some other prestigious school, by right of birth, a bright Universalist, through luck and hard work, might get into a more modest educational institution. More often, the bulk of a Universalist's culture was achieved almost entirely through his or her own effort. Unitarians, at least in New England, inherited their churches from generations past. With very few exceptions Universalists created their own societies and built their own meetinghouses.[19]

Large edifices were erected in working towns such as Malden and Haverhill, Massachusetts, and were obvious signs of Universalist success.

Universalism also attracted poor people, as shown in the story of Eunice Connolly, a laywoman who encountered many tragic life circumstances in the mid-nineteenth century. Her life journey is depicted in *The Sea Captain's Wife: A True Story of Love, Race, and War in the Nineteenth Century* by Martha Hodes. Eunice Richardson was born white and working class in New England in 1831. After her father deserted the family, they moved to Manchester, New Hampshire, where she worked in the mills. In 1849 she married William Stone, who came from a Universalist family. He was a carpenter, much like the other men on her mother's side of the family, who were farmers, carpenters, shoemakers, and laborers. Before the war, they moved to Mobile, Alabama, looking for work. Once the war broke out, William became a Confederate solider and eventually lost his life in the conflict. Even before the war, William had been sick a great deal and unable to work. The lack of opportunity combined with the loss of family relationships left them financially and socially adrift in the South. As Hodes comments, "Poor folks can't indulge much."[20] Poverty-stricken once her husband went to war, Eunice returned north and sewed and cleaned for work, the kind of labor performed most often by Irish immigrants.

She found some religious solace when she was able to return to the Universalist church in Claremont, New Hampshire. Before she left for the South, she had been a church member in Manchester, where a remodeling in 1850 increased seating capacity to 1,000. Hodes notes that Universalists, like evangelicals, found followers in northern factory towns, but there was no Universalist church in the southern city of Mobile. Besides, Universalism was a faith that included all people, black and white, in its scheme of salvation. Once she was back north in Claremont, Hodes describes the church treating Eunice as one of its charity cases. The Universalist Samaritan Society brought her food and firewood, but Hodes says Eunice could hardly join their social circles when she was receiving handouts. While she never had to move to the poor farm, Eunice is an example of a Universalist who as part of the urban working poor found hope in a faith that promised her an assurance on the other side of this life. Despite her hardships, Eunice's Universalist gospel comforted her that "God does not require that our petition be couched in elegant and beautiful language." It taught that even the lowest and poorest soul could talk with God heart to heart.[21]

Later in life Eunice was rescued from poverty when she married a black sea captain. Hodes is unsure how Eunice found the courage to allow love to take its course across color lines but speculates that her Universalist faith may have helped as she translated its belief in spiritual equality into greater independence for women to pursue their own course of finding happiness. After the war, writers began to depict these kinds of relationships, including Louisa May Alcott, who wrote a story about a white woman falling in love with a man of African descent. The crossing of racial lines was very courageous and produced irrevocable conflict within Eunice's family. Unfortunately, the love story ended tragically when the couple and Eunice's daughter were all killed in a ship wreck. Despite her difficult life, Eunice found solace in her faith. Hodes says, "that by embracing the optimism of Universalism, she found a faith that prophesied a blessed ending to an increasingly disappointing sojourn on earth."[22]

We know the Universalist message of spiritual equality had a remarkable effect on the degree of women's activism. The number of Universalists grew tremendously in the 1840s, perhaps fueled by the large numbers of women who joined. Opportunities for church work increased, and in the late 1840s, the General Reform Association included two women officers. After that women began to appear as delegates to conventions. These opportunities led to an increased number of women preachers. Henry Bacon became editor of *The Ladies Repository*, which had the largest circulation of any Universalist periodical. Its banner described it as "devoted to the defense and illustration of Universalism and the Rights of Women." It consistently advocated for the extension of women's rights.

Adin Ballou provides a portrait of another Universalist type. Peter Hughes describes him as "the son of a well-to-do, but not rich, farmer." Designated for the agricultural life, Ballou wanted more than anything to go to Brown University to become a lawyer, but his father refused to provide the funds to educate him for "idleness." When Ballou stood up at their Christian Connexion meeting one day and announced that the next Sunday he would preach, he had a plan in the back of his mind to set out on his own as a minister. He could run the family farm during the week and preach at the Elder Ballou Meetinghouse on Sundays. Ballou was not able to get off the farm until he converted to Universalism and was disinherited by his father. Although he never received much formal education, his writing reflects extensive reading in the Bible and in the works of Shakespeare and Sir Thomas More.[23]

In 1839 Ballou wrote "A Standard of Practical Christianity," which reflected his nascent beliefs in pacifism, anarchism, and socialism. He adopted the philosophy of Charles Fourier, a French utopian socialist, and used it to formulate his own plan for an ideal society, or what would soon become the Hopedale Community. The central economic arrangements at the commune included joint ownership, equal pay, and limited profits. These ideals contrasted sharply to what later developed when George and Ebenezer Draper became majority share holders. They converted Hopedale from a socialist venture into a successful capitalist model industrial community in 1856. While Ballou went on to serve the Unitarian Church in Hopedale, the Drapers took advantage of a family invention that increased the efficiency of weaving on power looms. They had begun manufacturing loom temples in Hopedale in 1853.

Capitalism caused deep divisions in Universalism. George Pullman, a Universalist, was a railroad magnate who cut jobs and increased working hours, precipitating a violent strike in 1894. When he died in 1897, Charles Eaton said, "The Universalist Church is the child of the people, came up out of the soil, and industry has crowned her if she should be crowned at all." While some Universalists supported exploitive business practices, others responded to injustices, especially against women and children. This was especially true in Philadelphia, where William Heighton organized meetings at the Universalist churches to prevent exploitation of working people. A Universalist theology of human solidarity gave impetus for Heighton to call upon the clergy to "teach the absolute necessity of undeviating justice between man and man." A number of Universalists were involved in securing child labor laws, including Charles Leonard, who was the founder of Children's Day, a special celebration of children that was adopted by the entire Universalist denomination in 1868.[24]

The most famous of those farmers who believed that all people were worthy was a relatively obscure backwoods preacher named Hosea Ballou, distant cousin to Adin Ballou. In 1805 Hosea Ballou produced *A Treatise on Atonement*, the greatest theological work in Universalist history. It catapulted him to fame and leadership in the denomination, and eventually a pulpit was created for him in Boston. His *Treatise* is a reflection of a relatively uneducated, gospel preacher who felt his faith more than learned it. It should be read with an understanding of the Calvinist influence on Ballou's faith development. The Universalist perspective that he elucidated emphasized a human relationship to a loving God who wishes for all to be happy and ultimately redeems all. In this vision, people are not distinguishable from one another, nor judged as saved or unsaved. Rather than asking about the role of human will in being saved from damnation, Ballou's vision centered on discerning God's will for all of creation: How are we bound up together? The central theological concern for John Calvin, one of the major founders of Protestantism, was how humans needed to conform to

God's will and not their own strivings. This was Hosea Ballou's goal, too.[25]

Ballou was reared in a strict Calvinist background. His father, a native of Rhode Island, had moved the family to the backwoods of New Hampshire, and Ballou was raised the son of a "pious and devout preacher," who could be described as a New Light and a Separate Baptist. He won hearts not by reasoned discourses, but by personal experiences of ecstatic religion. The pietism came from Ballou's rural, relatively uneducated, folksy, evangelical, and experiential faith and was characteristic of his hill country Baptist heritage.

In the 1790s, while he was settled in Dana, Massachusettts, Ballou began corresponding with Joel Foster, the settled minister in nearby New Salem. They discussed future punishment. Although the theological argument was not settled, Foster at one point attacked Ballou as an uneducated preacher of a strange doctrine, asking, "Do you not discover yourself to be illiterate in a degree which is hardly pardonable in one who sustains the place of a public instructor?"[26] The Standing Order minister criticized the uneducated, lower-class Ballou as a buffoon who was not worthy of Foster's regard. On the title page of the correspondence, Ballou is referred to as an itinerant preacher.

Differences of style and class continued to divide Unitarianism and Universalism. Because of its emphasis on evangelical piety, the sovereignty of God, and salvation grounded in determinism rather than something an individual can achieve, Universalism cannot be stereotyped as a lower class form of Unitarianism. In one telling attack that reveals this dichotomy, Charles Chauncy criticized John Murray for his "plebeian egalitarianism." Ballou did come to adopt the use of reason and a Unitarian belief about Jesus, but this should not blur the vast differences between Unitarians and Universalists. Ballou's faith was based primarily on an immediate sense of the divine and not reason. Mark Noll, the author of *America's God: From Jonathan Edwards to Abraham Lincoln*, says that many new doctrines surfaced in the revolutionary period, and that most of these, including Universalism, reflected a radical evangelicalism in the tradition of the great revivalist George Whitefield.[27]

Ballou's mentor was Caleb Rich, the most important native founder of Universalism. He was also an ecstatic visionary. Universalists combed the scriptures but did not always find what they were searching for until they had some direct religious experience. It was not so much transmitted by theological discourse as by plain conversation among family and friends. It was a religion made for those who would rise in the world: There was room waiting for them at the top, in this world as well as in heaven.

Ballou was often disappointed in his relationships with Unitarians. In volume four of his unpublished "Gems of Thought," he wrote,

> The Unitarians contend earnestly for the liberality of exchanging desks with the orthodox, and yet will not themselves exchange, but in few instances, with their brethren the Universalists. . . . While they plead for liberality in persuading the Calvinists to exchange with them, they will not exchange with Universalists, although many of the people who pay them their salary, desire it.[28]

Despite the theological kinship, this refusal to exchange was based on class. The Unitarians were educated, and the Universalists were not. In fact, there is no evidence that the uneducated Ballou ever even met Channing, even though their respective churches were just blocks apart, and they were in Boston together for twenty-five years.

A consistent kind of condescension occurred when Unitarians encountered Universalists. Nathaniel Stacy, the great itinerant preacher in New York and Pennsylvania, was originally from New Salem, Massachusetts. His parents had migrated from Gloucester, where his father Rufus was a fisherman. In New Salem, he became a farmer but barely eked out a living. They affiliated with the First Parish Church there but only joined as half-covenant members. A short-lived Universalist society was formed in New Salem in 1800, the same year a Universalist convention was held in nearby Orange. The Stacys had concealed their true faith until then because being an open Universalist "called forth," Stacy said, "all the bitter censures, denunciations, and condemnations of the standing order." They promptly joined the new society. Not long thereafter Nathaniel characterized his new optimistic faith as having "youthful vivacity," and he fell under the tutelage of Hosea Ballou in nearby Dana, Massachusetts.[29]

These Unitarian denunciations of Universalists occurred not only in rural areas but also in most urban centers. Henry Whitney Bellows, often credited with being the first person to give Unitarians a congregationally based organization with the founding of the National Conference in 1865, had strained relations with the well-known Universalist preacher Edwin Chapin in New York City. After Chapin died, Bellows described him as a "thoroughly good fellow, devout, sincere, and wondrous eloquent. But he was *coarse*, & mingled so much that was doubtful and low tone, with his ordinary social intercourse, that I eventually gave him a wide berth." Bellows went on to say that Chapin was an "emotional rhetorician, who contributed nothing to the thought of this community" and did not preach very "*instructively.*"[30]

It would be easy to characterize this as sour grapes in the wake of the consolidation of the two denominations, where many Universalists felt swallowed by the Unitarians. But the evidence clearly shows that Unitarians viewed the Universalists as low class. In her memoir *A Vanished World*, Anne Gertrude Sneller tells how a family member characterized the difference between the two groups: "The Unitarians have always looked down a little on us Universalists as poor relations."[31]

Bressler writes that Ballou's early Universalist theology was an effort to improve Calvinism, "especially in its heavy emphasis on the sovereignty of God." Salvation for the individual is bound up in the community of the whole. "The main object in all that we do is happiness," Ballou posits, and "knowing that his own happiness is connected with the happiness of his fellow-men, which induces him to do justly and to deal mercifully with all men, he is no more selfish than he ought to be." Bressler claims that Ballou rejected the hierarchal social vision of the Arminians, or proto-Unitarians, who argued that a person could achieve salvation based on merit, complemented by God's grace. This new Universalist vision did not make distinctions between people: "One's lot was cast with the rest of the human race."[32]

Universalists did not believe that the human race was cast out on its own, mired in sin. Rather, the entire human family is drawn up into God's love in one moral community. This is a God that has created a world that is one organic whole, and other people are essential to our salvation. Ballou writes, "A man acting for his own happiness, if he seek it in a narrow circle of partiality and covetousness, his selfishness is irreligious and wicked."[33] It is not possible, in Ballou's theology, to win through any sort of competition; only through cooperation, which brings all into the circle of creation. His was a classless vision, without pedigrees or genealogies. The salvific goal was union with others, not personal fulfillment. "I neither expect nor desire perfect happiness while I see my fellow-man in misery," he says. Virtue is always conceived of in terms of relationship, not in terms of self. Ballou continues, "The more humble we are the greater our enjoyments. But when we are completely humbled and perfectly reconciled . . . I believe all strife concerning who shall be great in the kingdom of heaven will be at an end."[34]

Central to Ballou's thought is that the misery of others, no matter who they are, does not secure personal salvation. In fact, as long as people lack humility before the creation and only grapple selfishly for personal salvation, God's goodness and plan for everyone is harder to understand. Ballou's God loves all and judges none. Sin is intended to achieve God's purpose, which is happiness found in reconciliation with God. Ballou does not deny the existence of sin, and in fact, human selfishness results in punishment for sins instantly and inevitably. Because sin is punished here, God's love is not selective in the hereafter, and thus there are no distinctions in heaven. Those who believed that people of the finest character were more likely to achieve salvation found this idea especially disturbing. A good, moral Unitarian did not want to share space in heaven with a prostitute. The orthodox said that sinfulness is infinite in our nature because of Original Sin, but Ballou believes sin is finite, as it represents the acts of finite beings.

After death, there is no such thing as distinctions among souls: All are in heaven, and all are loved. Since you are already saved, there is nothing you have to do.

Ballou spent the rest of his life defending his theology and refining his position that sin brought its own punishment in this life. The controversy with the Restorationists (those who believed in a period of punishment following death so that the soul could be purified) lasted for years. Some attacked Ballou on the grounds that his promise of freedom from punishment in the afterlife encouraged immorality in this life. Yet he remained firm that the quest for individual salvation was selfish, and like the orthodox New Divinity theologians, he said that human interests must be linked with the whole of humanity.[35]

Yet his viewpoint was not the predominant one after 1850. The distinctiveness of Universalist theology was adopted by the culture at large as Calvinism gave way to a more generalized Arminian philosophy, which posited that anyone can earn his or her way into heaven. With the gates open to all who lived worthy lives, the pressure to suggest that sinners endure at least some period of retribution increased.

By the end of the nineteenth century Unitarians and Universalists were more and more alike. In 1899 Willard Selleck wrote in *The Universalist Leader* on "What is the Difference between Universalism and Unitarianism?" He noted that a convergence had occurred with respect to class, scholarship, and theology.[36] Selleck implies that by the turn of the century you could not tell the difference between the two, except that Universalists were more interested in theology and things spiritual and that a conservative Universalist might be uncomfortable around a radical Unitarian.

In her book, Bressler reminds us of the standard differences usually depicted between the two groups. While both are grouped as liberal religionists, one is seen as an elite, the other as a more rustic, less intellectual counterpoint. She says this has some validity but Universalism has suffered by being depicted as Unitarians' poor relation.[37] This is unfortunate because demographically and socially Universalists actually lived out the values expressed in their faith of freedom and equality. A diversity of classes participated, and many members, especially before 1850, saw a classless vision of both heaven and earth. Universalist congregations welcomed both rich and poor, businessman and seamstress alike.

The elite Unitarians found the actual embodiment of the tenets of their democratic faith much more difficult, and this remains a challenge to Unitarian Universalists today. How do we live out a faith where all are truly welcome? Who is our message for?

When John Murray was preaching in Pennsylvania, New Jersey, and New York in 1773, he reported, "All my friends were to be found among every class of people, from the highest to the most humble."[38] All classes understood him. How can we, like one of our founders, learn to make friends among all classes and not just among those educated elite who are so much like us?

Scientific Salvation

F ROM THE EARLIEST days of Unitarianism and Universalism, these traditions have advocated for the compatibility
of science and religion. Both traditions encourage the use of reason, the search for truth, and the improvement of human nature
and society through learning and the discoveries of science. Some,
especially those called humanists, eschew Biblical revelation and
supernaturalism and believe that science and technology will eventually solve all the major problems facing humankind.

At the end of the nineteenth century, many liberals saw hope
in the new science of eugenics as it embodied a kind of evolutionary optimism. Many believed that the births of stronger, smarter,
and even more attractive babies would signal the coming salvation of the world. In the ensuing decades prominent religious liberals such as educator David Starr Jordan, jurist Oliver Wendell
Holmes Jr., and clergyman William Francis Potter became enthu-
siasts for eugenics. Their stories reflect our faith in science and
how our hopes for a better world can result in gross violations of
human freedoms and rights.

Unitarian Universalists today—who uphold the inherent worth
and dignity of every person as their first Principle—would be
shocked to read the title of a book published in 1902 by the American Unitarian Association: *The Blood of the Nation: A Study of the*

Decay of Races Through the Survival of the Unfit. The author was David Starr Jordan, president of Stanford and the most renowned ichthyologist in America.

During the early twentieth century, Jordan became the most sought-after speaker at Unitarian events. Between 1902 and 1916, he published nineteen books with the denominational imprint, Beacon Press. He was its most prolific author with most of his titles remaining on the Beacon backlist until the eve of World War II.[1] Jordan was an early advocate of evolutionary science, publishing many books and articles on the subject, including *The Relationship of Evolution to Religion* in 1926. He was also a prominent peace activist, a declared pacifist who wrote numerous articles for *Unity*, the periodical founded by his friend, Rev. Jenkin Lloyd Jones. By background and even name, David Starr Jordan seemed to be the ideal spokesperson for liberal religion. He was brought up in the Universalist faith and adopted his middle name out of his family's respect for the great Universalist and Unitarian minister who saved California for the Union, Thomas Starr King.

Yet this man with seemingly impeccable liberal religious credentials and convictions used science in troubling ways. Jordan's pacifism was based on a belief that war is a biological evil: It kills off the physically and mentally fit and leaves behind the less fit. He declared that poverty, dirt, and crime produced poor human material. "It is not the strength of the strong but the weakness of the weak which engenders exploitation and tyranny," he wrote in *The Heredity of Richard Roe.* Weak people bring failure upon themselves and ultimately will bring failure upon the nations they live in, if they are the ones who survive and reproduce.[2] War, Jordan believed, robs the race of its most vital blood.

Jordan's idea of promoting peace to preserve the best blood of the nations had its origins in eugenics, the most enduring aspect of Social Darwinism. Commonly referred to as the "survival of the fittest," Social Darwinism was a biological generalization applied to social forces at work in the world, made popular through the philosophical works of Herbert Spencer. Darwin's cousin, Francis Galton, coined the term *eugenics* in 1883 with the central idea that disease, poverty, and immoral behavior are largely determined by inheritance. In this theory, mass immigration would lower the standard of American intelligence, and national salvation was dependent upon preserving the racial stock. The poor were seen as biologically deficient, and the upper and middle class—especially white Anglo-Saxons—were superior people, both mentally and morally. This gave Americans a scientific rationale for their fear of the poor and immigrants—they could ruin the country.

In *The Blood of the Nation*, Jordan writes, "In the red field of human history the natural process of selection is often reversed." The unfit survive a war because it is "the fair, the brave, and the strong," who are sacrificed for the nation. If the best are lost in war, then "the nation in time would breed only second-rate men." This would lead to a degeneration of a people and the subsequent decline of the nations. Jordan continues, "Indiscriminate charity has been a fruitful cause of the survival of the unfit. To kill the strong and to feed the weak is to provide for a progeny of weakness."[3]

Jordan never adopted the extreme position of advocating the intentional development of a super race. In *The Heredity of Richard Roe, A Discussion of the Principles of Eugenics*, he states that nations were reversing the process of natural selection, as charities perpetuated the weak, war eliminated the strong, and education made celibacy a condition for success.[4] He claims that if the human race could control mating, then society could standardize strength, beauty, endurance, or virtue. Yet he contends that the best men would never submit to this kind of control. The best would want to choose their mates, and this was also better for society. If scientists chose mates for people based on the best bloodlines, they would exclude the two most important factors in mating, love and initiative. Descendants of such mates would not know the meaning of love. Still, Jordan's moderate position of positive eugenics in his writings implied that the stronger, more heroic races would produce better babies, while the weaker and less intelligent people who were surviving the wars would slowly destroy the human race with their inferior stock. It is a short step to the belief that inferior people should not reproduce ("negative" eugenics) and perhaps should not be allowed to live at all if the human race is to progress.

In *The Blood of the Nation*, Jordan says that the Roman Empire fell because war took all of their strong men. Only the cowards survived, and the new generations came from their blood. He notes that all of the great nations fell because they "bred real men no more. The man of the strong arm and the quick eye gave place to the slave, the pariah, the man with the hoe, whose lot changes not with the change of dynasties." Jordan's pacifism was founded upon pseudoscientific principles that nature would select the brightest from the best blood to continue the race, but war took those who would naturally rise to the top and left humankind with the dullest races instead.

Jordan was not especially comfortable with organized religion, preferring an individual rather than collective religion. He wrote that a person's education was not complete until it was "built about a pantheon, dedicated to the worship of great men." In *Life's Enthusiasms* he says that religion should be known by its tolerance, its broadmindedness, its faith in God and humanity, and its recognition of the duty of action. His belief that religion was based on a dedication to man's highest purposes made him a natural choice to be a philosophical spokesman for the American Unitarian Association.[5]

As a young man, Jordan found Darwin's theories of evolution difficult to accept. His mentor, Louis Agassiz, the prominent natural historian and Unitarian, opposed evolution, despite being a tireless promoter of science and an important theorist on the classification of species. Agassiz was also the foremost promoter of polygenism in the nineteenth century. Polygenists posited the creation of multiple human races, not one. They theorized that different races came to life separately in a series of different creations. The separate races were entirely different animals with different abilities. Polygenists were against racial mixing, saying it would create an effeminate offspring unable to maintain American democratic traditions.

Evolutionary theory required a belief in monogenesis, a common origin for all humans. Many liberals were slow to accept evolution, including the Universalists at Lombard College, who objected when Jordan taught the students about geological ages. He left under a cloud. Nevertheless, Jordan went on to a highly successful academic career and became the first president of Stanford in 1891. He embraced evolutionary theory and by the turn of the century Darwin's scientific importance was more fully appreciated, although Agassiz continued to reject evolution.

On the centennial of Darwin's birth, Jordan spoke about Darwin's influence at the Unitarian Club of San Francisco. Despite their scientific differences over evolution, Agassiz and Jordan maintained some common ground regarding the perceived different abilities of cultures and races.[6]

Advocating the physical and intellectual superiority of some people over others seems at odds with liberal religious principles. Many late-nineteenth-century Unitarians believed in the power of education to produce an enlightened and even ennobled society. The two men most often associated with the development of the educational system in America, especially in Massachusetts, are Horace Mann and Samuel Gridley Howe.

Mann helped transform the state's system of normal schools—which were really charity schools for the poor—into the modern system of free public schools, organized on principles that promote the natural curiosity and goodness found in every child. This philosophy came directly from his faith and ran counter to the predominant school methodology, which reflected a belief in the child's sinful nature and rewarded the child with widespread corporal punishment. Mann advocated for universal education, which he saw as the "great equalizer of the conditions of men." He said that if education were "universal and complete, it would do more than all things else to obliterate factitious distinctions in society."[7]

Mann and his friend Howe believed that society had created schools that expected and promoted the worst in human conduct because of their ideas about human nature. Howe's work was more specialized than Mann's, especially with Laura Bridgman, the first deaf and blind person to learn language. Howe saw Laura as an example of pure human nature because there were no external

influences to corrupt her. Believing that all people deserve the right
to be educated to reach their fullest potential, Howe achieved amazing results with Laura. His work with her helped develop what
later became the Perkins School for the Blind. She also became
world-famous and a lucrative sideshow for Howe's theories.

The major problem Howe encountered with Laura was her
showing natural impulses like anger, rage, and envy. These emo-
tions did not reflect his Unitarian theology of natural goodness.
No human being is as angelic as Howe hoped Laura would be. But
in many ways she proved his theory that when given the best
possible environment and an opportunity to develop, amazing
things can happen. Laura showed an incredible curiosity and an
ability to learn. Her progress is described in *The Education of Laura
Bridgman: First Deaf and Blind Person to Learn Language* by Ernest
Freeberg. Howe's belief that all people should be given the opportunity to develop to their fullest intellectual capacity was also
reflected in the philosophy of America's first institution for the
so-called feeble-minded, which he founded in Boston in 1848.
Howe said those who were once called untrainable could lead
independent, productive lives. In 1887 the Massachusetts School
for Idiotic and Feeble-minded Youth, later known as the Fernald
School, moved to Waltham.[8]

Although Howe's methods continued to be effective, his theories were called into question as scientists started to believe that
intelligence, character, and morality were all biologically based.
That meant the students in these schools could never be trained
to be on their own. If left to their own devices, they would produce mentally deficient people who would be a drain on society.
The Jukes, one of the earliest influential books that helped spread

public alarm, was written by an amateur criminologist, Richard Dugdale. He said that most of society's problems could be blamed on a wildly breeding underclass. The solution to these problems was the new movement called eugenics, meaning "good in birth."[9] "Positive" eugenics urged healthy white couples to have more babies. The birth rate for upper-middle class white women had declined, and this movement encouraged these women to become good breeders. "Negative" eugenics tried to assert that those who were not worthy to have babies should be discouraged, even prevented, from doing so. The Black Stork, a film made in 1917, carried the explicit message that babies born with birth defects should be killed. Death was the preferable solution for those who were weak or inferior.

While this policy was too radical for implementation, politicians began to respond to the eugenics lobby by turning state schools into prisons where the genetically "inferior" could be confined forever. Howe's idea of educating all to their fullest potential was considered ill-advised by Walter Fernald, for whom the successor school to Howe's was named. Fernald said even the brighter feeble-minded children would produce "degenerate children."[10] Thus began a campaign to place every American "moron" (a category determined by IQ tests), the new public danger, in a secure facility. This was replicated in many states. States could not afford to build enough facilities to house all those who were deemed unworthy. Here political eugenics came into play, with a push for state laws to sterilize those who were on public assistance and those who would breed children who would become wards of the state.

It worked. State after state passed new sterilization laws. The unfit were thus prevented from passing on their genetic heritage.

The best and brightest of progressives in the early twentieth century were allied to encourage fitter families and to discourage the birth of those who would be a burden on the rest. It was a progressive's personal, civic, and religious responsibility.

Looking at the vast immigrant populations, organizations turned to the new science of heredity to craft a more manageable, wholesome future. Many liberal-minded leaders came to believe that society could best advance if the genetic stock became progressively more intelligent, and so they embraced eugenic science. The legal highpoint of the eugenics movement was a Supreme Court decision in the case of *Buck v. Bell* in 1927, when Unitarians Oliver Wendell Holmes Jr. and William Howard Taft voted with the majority, with Holmes writing the decision.

This infamous decision was the culmination of the 1924 testing of a new Virginia law. Carrie Buck was scheduled to be sterilized under the new law. She had been raised in foster care, been raped, become pregnant, and given birth all before the age of seventeen. She was considered part of a "shiftless, ignorant and worthless class." The judge ruled the operation should be done. Appeals eventually took it to the Supreme Court.

Chief Justice Taft, who would soon serve as the president of the National Unitarian Conference, was already a supporter of eugenics. In 1913 he had become a board member (later chairman) of the Life Extension Institute. He played a prominent role in the publication of *How to Live*, a booklet that recommended healthy lifestyles and hygiene infused with eugenics ideology. It recommended that every state have eugenics boards with the goal of preventing "reproduction by the markedly unfit," and the sterilization of "gross and hopeless defectives." The book sold 133,000 copies and prominently displayed Taft's picture, reflecting his general support for eugenics policies. But when it came to rendering a written opinion on the Buck case, that fell to Holmes.[11]

Oliver Wendell Holmes Jr. was the most famous judge in America. His father, a poet and physician, provided a eugenics lesson when he declared, "A man's education should begin with his grandparents." Holmes failed to see how any "degenerate" could be improved or reformed. Following Herbert Spencer's philosophy on the survival of the fittest, Holmes said that science should "take control of life, and condemn at once with instant execution what is now left to nature to destroy." While the Unitarian tradition had affirmed a belief in the power of education to morally uplift all people, Holmes thought that those who "talk of uplift," affirmed a "squashy sentimentality that denied the predatory nature of the universe."

By the time of the *Buck v. Bell* Supreme Court case, more scientists were speaking out against a systematic legal means of eugenic sterilization, but Holmes did not adopt these views. Perhaps remembering his own sacrifice in the Civil War—he was wounded three times—and those of others, Holmes called upon Carrie Buck to do her part. He wrote,

> We have seen more than once that the public welfare may call upon the best citizens for their lives. It would be strange if it could not call upon those who already sap the strength of the state for these lesser sacrifices. . . . It is better for all the world if, instead of waiting to execute degenerate offspring for crime, or to let them starve for their imbecility, society can prevent those who are manifestly unfit from continuing their kind. . . . Three generations of imbeciles are enough.[12]

In his opinion, Holmes emphasized that Buck was a feeble-minded woman who came from defective stock. Arguing that the state had the prerogative to uphold a wider welfare in sterilizing mental defectives, Holmes assured the public that Buck had received due process. But she had not. Moreover, like thousands of others who were sterilized, she had none of the hereditary defects with which she had been labeled.

Many presumptions were made in this case about a lower-class woman who was a rape victim. In fact, no direct evidence showed that Carrie's baby, Vivian, was mentally defective. Nevertheless, Carrie was forced to make this "lesser sacrifice" of state-enforced coercive surgery.

Holmes was once called the "champion of the Common Man," but historian Paul Lombardo says that if Holmes ever had sympathies for the lower classes, he had lost them long before he wrote the opinion in the Buck case. In fact, he believed that society was better off if these "defectives" were not around at all.

These actions of state-enforced sterilizations violated basic human rights and specifically targeted the poor and disabled. While we acknowledge the misguided use of science then, we also must remember that it was an attempt to solve society's problems of crime, poverty, and disease with the hope of creating a better world. Even today we ponder how science might help or hinder our hopes of having healthy children as we confront issues of cloning and "designer babies."[13]

While the Buck case represents the most notorious case in the legal implementation of eugenics, many other campaigns and movements had eugenics components. Two issues that we often associate with liberal ideas of freedom of choice, birth control and euthanasia, had some of their foundations built upon coercive, class-based efforts to prevent defectives from being born or from being allowed to live.

In the early 1920s progressive high schools and YMCAs took part in a keeping fit campaign that exemplified "well-born science." The caption on one poster for the program read: "What kind of children?" The poster went on to explain that children get their basic qualities by inheritance. If they are to be strong, efficient, and great, "There must be good blood back of them." Youth had to think about the good blood of a future mate, if they wanted to stem what Margaret Sanger, the leader of the birth control movement, called, "unthinking and indiscriminate fecundity."

The campaign reflected some key questions. How many children should parents have? How can we ensure that only genetically fit children are born? What kind of children will give us a more perfect union?

Early in the twentieth century, those concerned with making fecundity more discriminating turned to birth control as a means to prevent births by those likely to breed and produce less than desirable children. Sanger saw similarities between the birth control movements and euthanasia, saying that "one being to bring entrance into life under control of reason, and the other to bring the exit of life under that control."[14]

In her *Autobiography* Sanger speaks of her relationship with the eugenics movement. "The eugenicists wanted to shift the birth control emphasis from less children for the poor to more children for the rich. We went back of that and sought first to stop the multiplication of the unfit. This appeared the most important and greatest step toward race betterment."[15] Like other eugenicists,

Sanger felt that the poor and the ignorant added to the severity of social problems, and therefore targeted them as women who needed to be prevented from reproducing.

The freedom of choice liberals often proclaim as a basis for faith became a repressive means of social control for others. Birth control was an important issue for the Universalists. In 1927 when they first appointed a committee to study birth control, the resolution called for an investigation into birth control and its relationship to "marriage, and the welfare of the race." They claimed to be the first denomination in the country to go on record favoring birth control when they passed a resolution in 1929, the same year that Margaret Sanger's birth control clinic in New York was raided.[16]

In 1916 William J. Robinson published *Fewer and Better Babies: Birth Control; or The Limitation of Offspring.* This combined information on the means of birth control with Spencerian "survival of the fittest" ethics and overpopulation issues. Some leaders were concerned about the number and type of babies to be allowed to be born, and this spilled over into how many immigrants to allow into the country. What kind of class judgments are still expressed by overpopulation advocates about families of more than two children?

In the early twentieth century, progressives, including a number of Unitarians, were very enthusiastic about eugenics. Kenneth MacArthur of the Federated Church in Sterling, Massachusetts, argued that decent Christians have a responsibility to use "every help which science affords" to prevent the "feeble-minded and wrong-willed from pouring their corrupt currents into the race stream." Clergy inspected prospective couples for marriage to make sure they were normal physically and mentally. The great Unitarian activist John Haynes Holmes, who worked with Margaret Sanger, encouraged his fellow ministers in the Liberal Ministers Association of New York to perform nothing but health marriages, or the conservation of the "normal" family, so that, in the interest of improving society, "defectives" did not propagate. He wrote,

> Nothing is more important, to my mind, in our modern treatment of the question of marriage, than to use our powers of social control to prevent many people from marrying—those, namely, whose marriage, for one reason or another, can be nothing but a tragedy.[17]

Holmes's interest in promoting eugenics seems to contrast with his social ideals. He once declared socialism the religion of Jesus. He believed in the struggle of labor versus capital and claimed that historically Unitarian churches had sided with capital. Labor union advocacy, he said, was an alien element in Unitarianism as it perceived itself as a middle class institution having high standards of respectability and culture and not a place where poor immigrants organized. Unlike other Unitarian churches, Holmes's congregation became a multicultural institution with rich and poor, black and white, a community church in the true meaning of that word.

Perhaps we should not be surprised that limiting who could marry was labeled a social good. When the Universalists passed their Declaration of Social Principles in 1917, its working program included the following: "We want to safeguard marriage so that every child shall be born with a sound physical, mental, and moral heritage."

Birth control or even sterilization were ways to control indiscriminate breeding. When Clarence Russell Skinner, the great Universalist social activist, published *The Social Implication of Universalism*, he declared,

> The new enthusiasm for humanity readily pictures a time when through eugenics, education, friendship, play, worship, and work, the criminal will be no more, because the misdirection or the undevelopment of human nature will cease."[18]

Skinner spoke of Universalism's quest for brotherhood, and yet his plan was to weed out the "criminal" element, at least partly through eugenics.

Throughout the United States sermon contests were held on the subject of better breeding. Sponsored by the American Eugenics Society, the contests had a central theme, "Religion and Eugenics: Does the Church Have Any Responsibility for Improving the Human Stock?" One participant in 1928 was Homer Gleason of the First Universalist Church in Rochester, Minnesota. He wrote to the society,

> Please allow me to add that I have greatly enjoyed my preparation for this work. I have thought for years that I was somewhat of a eugenist, but five months of intensive study have thoroughly convinced me. . . . Surely, this is a great cause.[19]

These contests flourished between 1923 and 1930 when the society increased the popularity of eugenics with contests and competitions among "fitter families" at state fairs. To go along with the largest pigs or cows, the fairs had the most racially perfect families on display.

Many progressives were also organizing to restrict immigration of what they perceived as inferior peoples. They declared a need to preserve the white, Anglo-Saxon, Protestant heritage in the face of new lower classes of immigrants, especially those who were not Protestants. In 1927 Andre Siegfried, in *America Comes of Age* asked, "Will America Remain Protestant and Anglo-Saxon?"

Americans prided themselves on their original stock. They promoted unity of the spirit by insisting that their center of gravity lay in their Anglo-Saxon and Puritan heritage. One day they might find that their stock would be diluted, and their distinctiveness as a people lost forever. This idea was blended with progressive religion. A certain set of citizens saw themselves as an elite, "moral aristocracy." They knew what was best for America. Historian Martin Marty describes them as being against cigarettes, alcohol, and slums and for feminism, pacifism, antivivisectionism, Americanization of immigrants, and even eugenics, birth control, and euthanasia.[20]

Sterilization and birth control were joined in the eugenics program by those who promoted euthanasia as another kindred cause. Charles Francis Potter, a Unitarian minister who quit the Unitarian movement, was the first president of the Euthanasia Society of America. Historian Mason Olds characterizes Potter as the "rebel of humanism."[21] He is an important figure in Unitarian Universalist history, as one of the founders of the humanist movement, along with John Dietrich and Curtis Reese. Potter's varied career included being the defense expert on the Bible at the Scopes trial and speaking in a series of debates against fundamentalist preacher

John Roach Stratton, held in Carnegie Hall. Potter published a number of books and tried to organize humanism outside of the Unitarian denomination. He affirmed the claim of Harvard Divinity School's Dean Sperry: that just as Unitarianism was a logical development from Protestantism, Humanism was a similar development from Unitarianism. Potter was also a signer of the Humanist Manifesto in 1933, as he believed that a new religion must arise to meet humanity's expanding needs. This was a faith in which people must believe in their own potential and dare to develop their own personalities. This coming faith had to include, incorporate, and intelligently use science, instead of fighting it as orthodox religion would.[22]

Potter claimed that as a pastor he had seen too many instances in which parishioners died in agony, and he saw euthanasia as a humane way for people to gain some control over their own deaths. He insisted that suffering incurables have a right to request and receive a merciful and painless release when death is inevitable.[23] He first announced his support for euthanasia in 1936 before the newly organized First Humanist Society of New York. He then formed the National Society for the Legalization of Euthanasia in 1938. He wrote that "euthanasia is an important social measure in the same class as birth control and eugenics."[24] Unitarian Universalists today generally support the freedom of choice in certain circumstances regarding control of our own deaths, and also want to prevent undue suffering—but Potter initially argued for a more widespread understanding of euthanasia.

While Potter declared that euthanasia relieved suffering and empowered individuals with some control and choice over this most trying part of life, he argued that it could serve social purposes as well. In 1936 he wrote that handicapped infants and the incurably insane and mentally retarded ought to be mercifully executed. He said people were being "special cowards" by not executing these "imbeciles," as a socially desirable act.[25] The *New York Times* reported that Potter had said the state could save $30 million that was wasted on the support of such people. He wrote, "I think it would be vastly more moral to kill off the incurable imbeciles and use the money for the children of the State than it would be to maintain the present absurd expenditure for their upkeep."[26]

The question about which type of euthanasia to advocate for was a central issue for the Euthanasia Society. In his autobiography, Potter says this was often debated and perennially discussed by board and society members. Should legislation be passed that permitted euthanasia for cases of congenital idiots and the incurably insane? Apparently, the majority of members, backed by physicians, favored voluntary euthanasia for the terminally ill over the larger social solution, first advocated by Potter, of mercy killing for people who suffered from mental illness or cognitive disabilities. Historian Ian Dowbiggin writes, "From Potter's perspective, involuntary euthanasia also paved the way for an 'ideal society' by eliminating undesirable defectives."[27]

Few people today would support the execution of these "defective" targets in a system of social engineering that promotes fewer and better births. Yet to achieve a society that allows the fullest development of personality in educational, social, and economic contexts, many reformers believed that progress could be best achieved by removing those people who are less desirable, less fully developed, or less intelligent—by means of birth control, abortion, or sterilization. If their births could not be prevented, then euthanasia could be permitted to achieve an ever-improving society.

Like other eugenics advocates, Potter saw "defectives" as a burden on society. They prevent us from making progress. They are at the margins and will always be so. Potter rejected the traditional Unitarian advocacy of individual freedom of choice to support a scientific and paternalistic system that controlled society in order to advance it. Potter had faith that scientific engineers could help decide the appropriate "number and quality of births."

In 1933 he delivered a radio address on NBC called "A Message to America," in which he said that humanistic religion "concerns itself particularly with the growth of the higher consciousness or personality of man, socially and individually, believing that man is potentially able by his own efforts to attain to the complete and perfected personality to which all religion aspires." He said that humanity had already accomplished wonders, and that "mechanical progress has been paralleled by social and economic, yes, even by spiritual progress."[28] Promoting the improvement and perfection of the self in an ever-progressing society could lead to the belief that "defective" people who could not be "improved" should not be here at all.

Potter was not alone. Inez Celia Philbrick was a doctor, professor, and Unitarian who served on the first Euthanasia Society board. From her office in Lincoln, Nebraska, she tried to win, but ultimately failed to gain, support for the nation's first euthanasia law. Socially she supported suffrage for women, birth control, eugenic sterilization, world peace, and an end to child labor. She said the commandment, "Thou shalt not kill," really meant thou shalt not commit murder. Mercy killing, religiously speaking, was not murder. She often attacked Catholics for calling suffering a blessing in disguise. Catholics were generally not part of the eugenics, birth control, or euthanasia movements.

Philbrick was brought into the euthanasia movement by a wrenching personal experience, but like Potter, she took it beyond an individual's right to choose to a much more horrifying idea of social control. She identified women as the guardians of the race. To be released from bondage, all mothers were responsible for seeing that no child was born with a handicap. She went on to argue that physicians had a responsibility to sterilize the unfit, a measure that alone could save civilization from annihilation. She believed that the removal of unworthy individuals was justified and merciful because they could not gain any satisfaction from living, and were a burden on society.[29] In contrast to Howe, who argued that all individuals should be allowed to develop as fully as possible with society's support, Philbrick claimed that no person who had a significant mental or physical disability could ever be happy. They will not have to suffer and have nothing to offer toward the advancement of society. Therefore, removing these people from life was a positive social contribution.

Beginning in the 1880s, many Protestant adherents of the social gospel saw the eugenics or "good birth" movement as an empirical method that would usher in the Kingdom of God on earth. The human condition could be improved with modern science through better breeding. It is disheartening to see that liberals, who were advocates for the advancement of science and the human race, were some of the leaders of the eugenics movement.

Other leading liberals used science and its methods in ways that promoted better understanding between races and classes.

Washington Gladden, leader of the social gospel movement, said that "Christianity must be a religion less concerned about getting men into heaven than about fitting them for their proper work on earth." Led by Congregational and Unitarian ministers, the social gospel movement reconceived Christianity as being less about faith and salvation and more about "ushering in the Kingdom of God on earth through social reform and service."

This effort to improve the human race and bring about the kingdom of God found its leading Unitarian proponent in Francis Greenwood Peabody. Peabody's father was a Unitarian minister who died in 1856, when Francis was nine. This made the subsequent years difficult, but the family found the means to educate Francis at Harvard College and then at Harvard Divinity School. Peabody was not impressed with his education though, saying, "I cannot remember attaining in seven years of Harvard classrooms anything that could be fairly described as an idea."[30]

His own ill health made the duties of a parish ministry difficult for him to pursue. He began to lecture at Harvard Divinity School and was appointed Parkman Professor of Theology. In 1886 he became Plummer Professor of Christian Morals, where he remained until his retirement in 1913. He was dean from 1900 to 1907. Peabody made a name for himself with the publication of *Jesus Christ and the Social Question* (1900), which eventually saw five editions. He felt the message of Jesus affirms that the test of salvation is the individual's contribution to social service.

His ideas helped develop an entirely new field of religious study, and he is often credited with being the first teacher in America to create a spot for social ethics in a course of university study and theological education.[31] He made this a crucial part of the education that prospective ministers received. His courses on ethics and social theory became known as "Peabo's drainage, drunkenness, and divorce." He believed that modern economic conditions were changing the social order, and political and economic problems must be considered ethical problems as well. Although he flirted with socialism, he never advocated a revolutionary change and instead tried to make the business community more virtuous. Seeing how widespread the problem was, Peabody advocated an ethic of justice and social democracy for all rather than old-fashioned charity for the poor. In 1909 he published *The Approach to the Social Question*, an interdisciplinary study.

The historian Barton Bernstein, in an article in the *New England Quarterly*, referred to Peabody as a conservative social reformer. His teaching helped rich, younger men, who may have felt separate from the masses, learn what industrialization had done to the poor. Children of privilege were given a sense of community obligation, and this helped to foment the Progressive movement. Peabody taught "the Christian duty of wealth, the need for charity, the evils of industrial competition, and the Christianity of cooperation."[32] Wealth, he said, must be used for social good. He criticized the old individualistic capitalism, which many Unitarians had affirmed as part of the fullest development of self. He wanted to abolish class hatred, and although he feared labor violence and strikes, he approved of unions. As a teacher, Peabody wanted his students to experience what life was really like. They wrote papers on slums and settlement houses, and they did field work in those slums where babies died in unheated tenements. He used new scientific methods to study and then act on social issues. These new methods included case studies and charts, and he especially tried to use photography to document social problems to make a stronger argument for reform programs. He founded a social museum at Harvard to house vast collections of photographs and studies, and the Phillips Brooks house, which promoted public service. Peabody tried to combine social science methodology, photography, and his religious faith to make substantive changes in society.

Generally, the Social Gospel sought change in the hearts of those with power and influence rather than in social structures. While socialism was too revolutionary for Peabody, he advocated the development of producer cooperatives to create a society based in brotherly love. He wrote, "A part of good citizenship lies in bearing others' burdens."[33] Peabody also supported construction of tenement housing for the working poor, as seen in the affordable housing project of Alfred Tredway White in Brooklyn. Peabody said the system of private ownership is a test of character calling for conscience as well as capacity:

> If . . . self aggrandizement and vulgar ostentation shall supplant simplicity and self-sacrifice as the habit of the prosperous, the capitalistic system—now under severe strain—is likely to be found wanting and to be displaced.[34]

He believed the rich man owes his wealth in a social obligation and issued a call for conscience. There is a "general struggle," he said, "for the existence of two types of civilization, one dominated by an interest in the development of the individual, the other characterized by a concern for the social order."[35] Like Peabody, Unitarians in general have historically struggled with the paradox that although they were advocates of reform, they preferred not to upset the social order. Peabody approved of some government activity in social betterment, but he believed that organizations were the channel through which human personality may work more effectively.[36] He was loath to weaken the sense of personal responsibility when it came to the cause of societal evils. Peabody was not the most radical of reformers, even lecturing his students that "economic inequality is the people's own fault." He approved of the individualistic, free enterprise system, and even to some extent, the accumulation of wealth, but there was a duty that went with wealth. He deplored capitalists like Carnegie, who said that the law of competition is best for the race because it assures the survival of the fittest. A rich man must regard himself, Peabody said, not as a "possessor but as a trustee, who is conscious of owing his wealth, as much as of owning it."[37]

Many Universalists also believed that wealth should be shared more equitably. George Williams reports that beginning in the mid-nineteenth century, Universalists advocated for better treatment of women workers in the textile mills in Lowell, Massachusetts. Abel Thomas and Thomas Baldwin Thayer organized improvement circles for women and published *The Lowell Offering* for educational enlightenment. In 1884 the Universalist General Convention focused on the prevention of cruelty to children and animals and passed a resolution on these issues in their plenary session. On the day before the Pullman Strike began in 1894, Universalist minister Levi Powers called for a more equitable distribution of wealth. He said that concentrating so much wealth in so few hands makes slaves of workers, who are mocked with the word *freedom* because their employer takes no responsibility for their welfare.

Universalists stood on both sides of this issue. When the railway car magnate George Pullman reduced his workers' wages twenty-five percent and yet continued to charge the same rates for rent, the socialist Eugene Debs came forward to lead the support for the workers. Pullman's brother James, a Universalist minister, affirmed what George Williams called "industrial paternalism." By the early twentieth century Clarence Russell Skinner at Tufts University was leading the Universalists to a deeper understanding that social problems are caused by unjust social and economic conditions rather than individual depravity. Skinner's "Declaration of Social Principles" called for a new economic and social order, where the gifts of God are shared, with "equal rights for all, special privilege for none."[38]

Today it probably surprises us that some Unitarians and Universalists supported eugenics. We generally think our faith empowers us to speak for those who otherwise have no voice and to advocate for those who cannot advocate for themselves. Yet the eugenics movement had about it, as Richard Hofstadter noted, the air of "reform." Like the progressive reformers, it accepted the principle of state action toward a common end and a better collective destiny, rather than individual development.[39] The individualism that had generated so much cultural change in the nineteenth century was giving way to a new collectivism.

Unitarians and Universalists who believed in eugenics or the social gospel had a more collective vision than religious liberals had ever had before. While the eugenics advocates wanted to minimize the impact or even eliminate the lower classes, other reformers like Peabody used their understanding of scientific studies to recognize the need for a greater sense of relatedness to one another, rich and poor, upper class and lower, in a broader social order.

In 1953, twenty years after *The Humanist Manifesto*, John Dietrich wrote that the Manifesto placed too much emphasis on science and reason. Seekers after truth, he said, should be more humble.[40]

In the wake of World War II, Clarence Russell Skinner gave voice to the realization that science had served "the ends of destruction." He said, "Our culture . . . has let science go where it will, serving heathen gods." In *A Religion for Greatness*, Skinner concluded that "we must come to grips with one of the great problems of our time: Will science freely lend itself to any form of evil which demands its service and pays it price?" Skinner was writing at a time when science had placed in human hands the ultimate weapon of destruction, but he also knew that creating life in test tubes was possible. We still wrestle with these questions of life and death in our time as science makes advances, and we experience limited resources and growing populations. It helps us to know what pathways we have trod before. Skinner concluded: "Science says to religion: 'Your goodness is not wholly good if it be not true.' Will religion have the courage to say to science, 'Your truth is not wholly true if it be not good?' That is a bold question."[41]

We must always address this question as we keep in mind the needs of the many, and not the few; the vulnerable, and not merely the privileged. And if we are people of privilege in some way, let us realize that we build a better world by recalling what we must share with others in an increasingly small world.

A Faith for a Few

M Y COLLEAGUE Patrick O'Neill wrote an article called "Why Unitarian Universalist Churches Close for the Summer." Reason number two reads: "It began with our New England roots. The Unitarian churches would all close down in the 1800s, and everyone headed for Cape Cod. The Cape churches stay open all summer."

When I served the First Parish in Milton, Massachusetts, a suburb south of Boston, we had no summer services. We assumed no one stayed in town for the summer. The wealthy congregation dispersed to their summer homes, or at least the wives and children did so, with the husbands to follow on weekends when they were free of obligations in the financial district. Perhaps this was more of a myth than a reality, but the tradition was still present.

In 1872, Ellen Tucker Emerson, Ralph Waldo Emerson's daughter, wrote to her sister Edith Forbes, reporting that she had safely landed back at the manse in Concord after a prosperous journey, and "remember our visit to Naushon with pleasure."[1] Her descendants in the Milton congregation planned their summer excursions to this same family island refuge. It is well known that summer congregations were much larger than winter ones in Brewster and Barnstable on Cape Cod and on Nantucket, only to return to fewer numbers as seasonal members headed home in September or early October.

In the book *Becoming Cape Cod*, historian James O'Connell tells how merchant Samuel Hooper bought a home in Cotuit in 1850. Other Brahmin families such as the Lowells were soon attracted to the area. Eventually, Cotuit became known as "Little Harvard," because so many professors summered there.[2]

While ecclesial think tanks have since informed us that closing churches in the summer is no way to run a growing church, the tradition has died hard. We joke that Unitarian Universalists are the only religious folk that God can trust to be free of divine oversight in the summer, but we also know that the church needs to be open and available every week. This is for visitors as well as for our members who do not happen to be wealthy enough to own a summer home in some exotic location.

We have long promoted ourselves as a democratic faith with a central belief that all people are welcome. From the beginning in Massachusetts, liberal Congregationalists said all have the right of private judgment in matters of faith, while they continued to affirm the need for a state church, which by its nature was grounded in coercion and privilege. They wanted a democratic society, but they believed they were the ones who were best equipped to lead that society and should determine its parameters. The ways in which we desire to improve the human race or increase individual control over our own destinies has resulted in projecting our vision of the good life onto others. Therefore, our ability to be compassionate toward marginalized people is limited. We want a democratic faith that embraces all, but in our efforts to extend this liberal religion, we frequently embrace only those who are like us.

After the Civil War, a campaign was begun by the American Unitarian Association to found churches in college and university towns. Virgil Murdock, former minister-at-large of Boston's Benevolent Fraternity, later reported that this "College Town Mission" program proved to be one of the association's most successful extension activities and included new congregations in Ithaca, New York, and Iowa City, Iowa.[3] We take particular note of the kind of communities that were targeted as potential areas of growth for the denomination. The plan was to evangelize highly educated people, or a cultured elite. But this proselytizing ended after the turn of the century, and extension efforts reached a low ebb in the early twentieth century.

In September 1946, the American Unitarian Association's minister-at-large, Lon Ray Call, delivered a memo called "A Research on Church Extension and Maintenance Since 1900: A Progress Report." He wanted to answer the question, "When and under what conditions should groups be encouraged to organize a new church?" He found what he called seven surprises. Two surprises were that the number of Unitarian congregations founded since 1900 had declined steadily, even precipitously, and that some of the best potential cities for new congregations had been overlooked. This, he surmised, was not purely based upon size but other factors as well. Call wanted to see where Unitarian churches had been successful before, but also the potential barriers to success. These included such factors as whether a liberal church was already present and "the percentage of foreign born and negro populations." Then he added other criteria as well, including how people make their living, what they read, and whether they are interested in culture and higher education.[4]

Using these criteria, Call picked forty cities that might be good areas for extension. University towns were typical choices, and his forty included Austin, Texas, and Durham, North Carolina. We could say that Call was merely being realistic in thinking that in the twentieth century our liberal faith always appealed to the white, upper-middle class professional who was highly educated. He thought Unitarianism would grow if we continued to reach out to those who are like us. Finally, after concluding that no well-founded policy of church extension had existed since 1900, Call refined his plan by suggesting that small groups of Unitarians be gathered in lay-led societies. This followed up on an American Unitarian Association board vote from 1945, which recommended that a plan be developed for forming lay centers.[5] The plan resulted in the greatest period of congregational growth in Unitarian history. This occurred in the 1950s and 1960s and came to be known as the fellowship movement.

In a "Report of the Department of Extension," delivered to the 123rd Anniversary Week Meeting of the AUA in May 1948, Call followed up on some of his earlier findings. As far as growing a faith that reflected more class and racial diversity, the report included some positive results. A new church had been formed on the south side of Chicago under the leadership of African-American minister Lewis McGee. Call noted that this church was interracial in reality, as all our churches are in theory.[6] Call also reported that many people were being either drawn or driven to Unitarianism by a reaction to the resurgence of orthodoxy. Other factors in the potential attraction to religious liberalism included the rise of intolerant bigotry, the decline of democratic values, and increased efforts to publicize the liberal faith.

Call said it was his task to bring the faith to brand new communities to introduce hundreds of people to Unitarianism. He said these people should come not only from the halls of universities but also "from the marts of trade, from factories (yes, from factories) and from kitchens and drawing rooms." He even went on to speculate that

[The Unitarian faith] is now growing most rapidly among those, sometimes without college training or often without any religious background, who look at you—you who have struggled up through years of college study, university research, tough wrestling with the spiritual implications of science and philosophy—and say . . . "I agree with you 100 percent."[7]

Aspirations to class diversity within Unitarian ranks is a mixed message. Our democratic faith preaches that all are welcome and aspires to having people from the factories join us. In theory, Call said, we should be racially diverse—but was there ever much of an intention to be so, or even a realistic expectation that it might be possible? The theory of democracy was not realized in the actual targets of extension.

Any history of Unitarian growth must acknowledge the importance of Lon Ray Call, especially to a movement that had seemingly lost its way in terms of extending the faith. As AUA minister-at-large, he founded thirteen churches. For his work devising the fellowship movement, he was given the name "the godfather of Unitarian fellowships." One of the churches he founded was the South Nassau Unitarian Church on Long Island in Freeport, New York, where he served as minister from 1951 until 1960.

Plans for extension on Long Island were especially pertinent for the class of people Unitarians expected to join their congregations at this time. In November 1946, Call wrote to George Davis, the AUA Director of Extension, reporting that Nassau County was of particular interest. Call said that in 1930 the percentage of white families filing personal income taxes there was 58 percent, much higher than New York State as a whole at 43 percent, or the United States generally at 22 percent. He added that the "main characteristic of the area is the large number of separate family houses of the upper middle class." He concluded that Nassau County was the best possible kind of district for Unitarian churches centering around the family.[8]

Dale Dewitt, the AUA regional director for New York, wrote Call and assured him that the movement would not grow on Long Island until there was some leadership, concluding, "I am sure there is a grand field there however."[9] Call's own ministry in Freeport culminated with an address about the prospects for merger that was reprinted in the AUA's minister's packet.

Call's sermon "Shall Unitarians and Universalists Unite?" is critical of the Joint Commission on Merger, partly based on his analysis of the differences between Unitarians and Universalists. The sermon reflected his concerns about who he felt was attracted to Unitarianism and where the expansion of liberal religion would prove most successful. While the commission noted that 60 percent of Universalist churches were in communities of less than 10,000 people, 60 percent of Unitarian churches were in communities that had populations in excess of 25,000. The commission concluded that this made the two groups complementary and therefore an advantage for consolidation, but Call thought it a disadvantage. He said that if the "mass of Unitarians are city folk and the mass of Universalists are country folk," then the "difference in the manner and mood of church life" between the two groups is more than the commission will admit.[10] Call went on to say that he wished the commission had considered this further, and that the consolidation would not solve but compound their problems. In a letter from Robert Raible to George Spencer in 1971, Raible recalled that Lon Call "vigorously opposed the Unitarians giving the Universalists any advice" on organizing fellowships.[11]

By 1960, Call had developed exacting standards for where he thought Unitarianism could expand. Call believed that fellowships could be organized in any type of community, but that places where they believed Unitarianism could flourish were preferred. Laile Bartlett, in her history of the fellowship movement, *Bright Galaxy*, describes a hypothetical but typical Unitarian fellowship. She places it in a Midwestern small college town, with the classic conflict between town and gown. The charter members were mostly from faculty families. Thus, in the town's sociological conflict, the Unitarian fellowship represents one part of the spectrum— a highly educated, white elite. Perhaps the makeup of the group reflects the obvious. It is not a democratic cross-section of the town, yet the purposes of the congregation state that it believes in "brotherhood undivided by nation, race, or creed, and allegiance to the cause of a united world community."[12]

Call put together the "Organizational Guide" for the fellowship movement. In it he said that Unitarianism attracts people from all walks of life, but then qualified that by stating that people in some professions are more responsive to liberal religion's appeal.

These included natural scientists, social scientists, architects and engineers, social workers, and modern educators.[13]

Munroe Husbands, the AUA's director of fellowships and associate director of extension, prepared a publication called "Organizing and Serving Unitarian Fellowships." He wrote, "Top consideration must be given to communities in which are located liberal arts colleges, for it has been easier to organize fellowships here than elsewhere."[14] Those places dominated by one or two industries were the least attractive.

While the AUA concentrated their extension efforts among those people characterized as having the best potential for membership, the AUA's Commission on Planning and Review, in a 1947 report, advocated for efforts to integrate people of color. The commission urged the appointment of a special committee "to study the policies of churches in relation to constituents and members from minority races."[15]

The extension policy and the commission's report seemed at odds with one another. While the report reflected the intention to establish more diverse, interracial congregations, the actual planning for extension ran counter to this. New suburban population centers challenged liberal religious thinking. As Bartlett noted,

> Most of the new communities are inherently and diametrically at variance with the liberal ideal of a broad spread of contact between a variety of people. While Unitarians engage in social action opposing class and racial discrimination, and in study of the world's people and their religions, those living in suburbia are increasingly isolated from the objects of their concern.[16]

The Fellowship Movement: A Growth Strategy and Its Legacy by Holley Ulbrich reiterates that growing college communities were "especially fertile ground for planting the Unitarian religious flag in new regions of the country."[17] New fellowships were religious homes for a growing number of academicians and an expanding population of educated professionals. These congregations were characterized by strong lay leadership. Of the congregations founded during the fellowship period between 1948 and 1967, 323 survive today—nearly a third of the total number of UU congregations. One of the earliest fellowships was in Stillwater, Oklahoma. Nearly all of its initial members were Oklahoma State University faculty and their spouses. Yet it was in the Northeast where the first wave of fellowships succeeded, despite the already large number of established churches. Ulbrich writes that this was because it had "more urbanization, suburban development, and commerce. It had a greater concentration of colleges and universities, and its residents had, on average, higher levels of education and income."[18]

The fellowship movement made a number of important contributions to our movement. Among those are a sense of shared ministry among the laity and the professionals and a vibrant sense of democratic leadership that challenges traditional authoritarian models—sometimes to the extreme of having no authority or tradition, only freedom. Bartlett suggests that a core concern for the fellowships was "how to capture true democracy in the fellowship operation."[19] Efforts to achieve consensus sometimes meant that congregations tried to avoid sharp differences, but this could make them conflict avoidant. The fellowship model helped institute more broad-based and diverse leadership patterns. Yet the empowerment of the laity did not lead to much diversity among the parishioners themselves. If anything, the prevailing pattern of catering to white, upper-middle class professionals was never challenged and was actually reinforced in the AUA's implementation of the expansion plan. This was also true of later efforts at expansion, including identifying potential areas of growth using zip codes that corresponded to wealthy, white, and well-educated population centers.

In their 2001 report, *Belonging: The Meaning of Membership*, the UUA Commission on Appraisal addressed this disparity between the ideal of pluralism and the reality of Unitarian Universalist congregations. While our Principles affirm that we would welcome someone who is very different from us, many of our members feel we should recruit among those who match the demographic characteristics of our current membership. New members should fit in or be like us for us to grow, and therefore there is little challenge to confront change.

From 1950 until 1960 many Unitarian congregations said they wanted to be diverse, and in theory had a faith that was open to all—or a "religion for one world," as Rev. Kenneth Patton once said. Yet the one world they promoted looked very much like themselves. What is most striking about our desire to be diverse today is that our multiracial and multicultural populations are usually the adopted children in our church schools, or the few adults among us who have the same education, income, and values as everyone else. Our yearning for diversity does not include differences of class. There is a long history of assumptions that people of different classes, cultural groups, and ethnic backgrounds would not be attracted to our rational, liberal faith. So our public expression of a democratic faith open to all does not find practical application among us. Therefore, the Commission on Appraisal concluded, our practice "does not always match the Principles we espouse."[20]

One way of looking at patterns of class structure among Unitarian Universalists is to see where and with which populations we intentionally tried to grow. Another perhaps more well-known pattern of bolstering the homogeneity of class is the "white flight" to the suburbs from the inner cities. Although we witnessed this in the mid-twentieth century, it was not a new phenomenon. In the 1850s Rev. Arthur Fuller dreamed of a more diverse Unitarian population in his pews because the North End of Boston, where his church was located, was a port of entry for first Irish and later Italian immigrants. But unfortunately, the New North Church building—the only surviving church in Boston designed by Charles Bulfinch—was sold in the 1860s to the Catholic diocese, and eventually the congregation dissolved.[21]

Time and again, congregations moved to where they perceived their people were moving. During Chandler Robbins' forty-one-year ministry at Second Church in Boston, the congregation had buildings in four sections of the city, finally ending up near the Brookline line in a neighborhood that was "opulent and residential." Yet the congregation eventually abandoned that location too, selling their 1912 Ralph Adams Cram building when business encroachments and apartment buildings made the neighborhood less appealing to a Unitarian congregation.

It is commonly assumed that the urban crisis in America began after World War II, when African Americans moved into the industrial cities of the North, and whites fled to the suburbs. Yet as we have seen, this transition started much sooner. It has become increasingly evident that the crisis of the city began when cities became places where poor people predominated. In the meantime, the automobile enabled the middle class to escape.

In his book *Urban Exodus: Why Jews Left Boston and the Catholics Stayed*, Gerald Gamm makes a compelling argument that some of the sociological forces behind this neighborhood transition were religious. Catholic institutions did not have to be concerned as much with market forces, and so the institutions were anchored in a sense of territorial place, under a bureaucratic hierarchy. Jewish synagogues, even though they were more tolerant, were governed by a different set of rules, more like the decision-making we might associate with Unitarian Universalist congregations. The decision to move or not depended entirely upon the people who made up the individual congregations and the competition for members. In a religious free market, the congregations went where they believed they would survive and prosper. I am not trying to judge whether these were good or bad decisions, but want to demonstrate what they did to survive and grow. While their decisions clearly reflect who Unitarian Universalists have traditionally believed "their people" were, they also show some desire to maintain a relationship with the populations who live in the poor, urban centers.[22]

Did fear of the city and its poverty and crime lead to a Unitarian Universalist exodus to the suburbs? We know that many downtown church buildings were abandoned. We also know that the new suburbs were targeted as appropriate places where liberal congregations could attract white, educated, upper-middle class people.

I am most familiar with the case of Springfield, Massachusetts, near where I grew up. The Third Congregational Society in Springfield was formed in 1819 because some of the richest, most established parishioners seceded from the First Parish Congregational Church. By the 1860s the congregation needed a new building, and a competition among architects was won by the soon-to-be-famous H. H. Richardson. His first commission was the Church of the Unity, erected downtown on State Street in 1869. At the time it was called "the most ambitious, the grandest, and the most satisfactory attempt at elaborate church architecture ever attempted" in Springfield. One-third of the final cost of $150,000 was pledged even before the plans were accepted, and at completion there were no unsettled obligations. For decades it was considered Springfield's most beautiful building. But over the next fifty years populations shifted, roofs began to leak, and finally, in 1957, the congregation voted to abandon it and relocate. In 1961, the building was torn down. A parking lot has been there ever since. A proposed hotel was never built.

As the Richardson church was being torn down, a new building for the congregation was constructed near the Longmeadow border, a prosperous suburb. Difficult to find and far from the center of the city, the Springfield church is an example of what happened in many other places.[23] As the congregation moved out of the city, the church members initiated an investigation into slum conditions, and plans for social action began in the same place they had recently abandoned.[24]

The destruction of the Springfield Church did not happen without a great deal of consternation. In 1953 AUA President Frederick May Eliot responded to correspondence from Eleanor Herrick of Norwalk, Connecticut, who was panicked over a *New York Times* article stating that the Springfield church was going to be abandoned. She had written to Eliot on June 28, saying that this was a "Richardson Church," where she was married, concluding that "The AUA just can't let this happen!" She recalled how this church was the wealthiest and most important church in the city. What happened?[25]

Eliot tried to reassure her that no plan was underway to give up the building and that despite "serious problems connected with the fabric of the present church building," the idea of selling it and moving elsewhere had been set aside.[26] Eliot told Ernest Sommerfeld, then the minister of the church, that he had persuaded Mrs. Herrick that "the entire Unitarian denomination has not as yet gone completely to the damnation bow-wows."[27] But perhaps it had. Despite a major renovation in 1935, the building deteriorated quickly. In the fall of 1951, the AUA's Grant Butler advised Sommerfeld not to repair the roof, put in new heating equipment, or do other maintenance until they knew for certain that there would be enough money to do so.[28]

Mrs. Herrick wrote back to Eliot on July 4, 1953, saying she was relieved that the alarming story in the *Times* was incorrect. But only a few years later, the building was condemned, and her fears about this once "largest and wealthiest group in Springfield" came to pass.[29] In 1961 the *Springfield Republican* announced that time had run out on the Church of the Unity. A farewell article in the paper said, "Within a few weeks the dismantling and razing will end the life of what has often been termed 'Springfield's most beautiful building.'" It said the church would soon break ground on its suburban site. The newspaper characterized the move as one that "exhibited the thread of Unitarian thought—daring to change, to experiment, to serve the needs of today for the good of tomorrow." The article concluded that the new building would be "a forward-looking example of . . . adaptation of machine age forms to the liberal quest for better ways for a better life today leading to a better life tomorrow."[30]

Was it better to abandon the downtown church? In 1990 the church printed a brochure called "Growth and Decision" that emerged from the UUA's Decision for Growth Program. In the summary of the Sommerfeld years, the brochure noted that moving out of the city center had consequences. One of them, further down the list, includes, "Negative community image resulted from tearing down church." In 1962 Alice Harrison, a UUA director for junior high programs in the education office, filed a report with the UUA stating that the Springfield congregation had a "new lease of life." While it did give the congregation a new, contemporary facility, membership fell from 306 in 1961 to 219 in 1991.[31]

The struggle between balancing a liberal, democratic faith that welcomes all kinds of people with a building location projected to attract people who are believed to be likely to help the congregation grow played out in many locations. One occurred in Berkeley, California. A Unitarian church had existed in Berkeley since the late nineteenth century, next to the downtown University of California campus. By the 1950s the congregation was already somewhat divided. A gift of land in Kensington, a relatively isolated neighborhood of the Berkeley Hills, had generated strong interest in moving out of downtown. As the university system tried to take ownership of the church building, a lawsuit ensued to ensure fair value for its purchase. The church won the suit and sold the building. The original church, built in 1891, became the property of the university and is currently a dance studio.

As building plans in the hills unfolded, some church members became dissatisfied with the new plan, others were dissatisfied with the minister, while some "shared a commitment to remain in the heart of Berkeley." As a result, sixty families left the First Church to form the Berkeley Fellowship of Unitarian Universalists, which was incorporated in 1957.[32] The fellowship acquired a building that was both adjacent to the campus and the downtown area. Curiously, the *History of the First Unitarian Church of Berkeley* mentions the split in the context of fund-raising and church planning, but nothing about having a downtown presence. And yet the fellowship lists its downtown presence as primary on its website.[33]

Despite the split in Berkeley, Unitarian Universalists were able to stay downtown as well as have a larger, new campus for an expanding congregation in a beautiful, natural setting that one local website tells you is admittedly hard to find. ("Get directions, you'll never find it.")

Another interesting example of a congregation's struggle to reach out to and speak to a wide range of people occurred in Cleveland, Ohio. In June 1951, the First Unitarian Church of Cleveland announced that a majority of their members had voted to move from their downtown location to Shaker Heights. The church Planning Commission decided that their primary objective had to be the overall growth of Unitarianism. Members of First Church, who had also established the West Shore Church in 1946, hoped that if they moved to the Heights, they would also maintain a downtown presence. They got their wish when 317 members of the First Unitarian Church decided to stay and so split off from the group that wanted to move. They believed an inner-city presence was important and purchased the building from First Church. They described the need to maintain a metropolitan religious society "which would be readily accessible to the lonely Sunday morning passer-by, the out-of-town stranger, the college student, the apartment dweller."[34] This congregation formally organized in 1951 as the Unitarian Society.

At first, this congregation had the kind of membership that a universal faith aspires to. They came from various cultural, economic, and racial backgrounds. The congregation was called a "Color-Blind Church" in an article in the *Cleveland Plain Dealer*. The article said that from the first day of worship, racial integration was never a problem, and the church became an example for the entire community. "Members of both races have prayed, studied, and worked together in complete harmony."[35]

Unfortunately this was a short-lived reality of our vision of the truly universal church. In 1969, a year after the Cleveland UUA General Assembly, the magazine *UUA Now* reported that the "ghetto church" was given to the Black Unitarian Universalist Caucus (BUUC). The property was turned over to thirty black members of the Unitarian Society for black community use. Hayward Henry of the BUUC said it was likely that other Unitarian Universalist congregations would give ghetto facilities to blacks, while white constituents moved elsewhere. Further, the article stated that the swing toward black solidarity has called "the integrated church into question."

Some of the same issues which exploded in the UUA's black empowerment controversy emerged in this situation. In that divisive conflict on the national stage, African-American Unitarian Universalists and their supporters sought UUA funding for black-run programs. But controversy developed around issues of black separatism, control of funds, and ultimately fiscal problems at the UUA. Before the property was given to the thirty black members of the Unitarian Society in Cleveland, church leadership continued to be white, and neighborhood blacks were not recruited or welcomed. Perhaps most enlightening, the *UUA Now* article continued, "Some blacks have resented 'outside control' and white presuppositions about how a church should function." Henry was quoted as saying, "Despite the pious rhetoric of brotherhood and justice, religious institutions have dismally failed to reconcile the contradictions between their pronouncements and practices."[36]

Whites became increasingly fearful of entering Cleveland's black neighborhoods. Some considered their giving up the church to be the abandonment of a dream, illustrated by the local Presbyterian minister, who called this action a "white, liberal cop-out." The BUUC was not able to maintain a fully functioning church facility. Eventually the building was torn down and replaced with a parking lot, reminiscent of the Springfield story. A little more than a decade ago, there was a proposal to form a new downtown church in Cleveland, called Urban Hope. The literal hope was that a downtown presence in a racially divided city could bring diverse groups of people together. On a more practical level, some felt that many people with Unitarian Universalist values lived in the inner city and wanted to build diverse community, search for justice, and empower the poor. We Unitarian Universalists continue to dream of a democratic free faith, although this project did not come to fruition.[37]

The episode raises some crucial questions about race and class diversity. Will leadership be shared? Can we grow and change beyond our own comfort level? Do we only welcome newcomers if they are like us? On whose terms does the life of the church unfold?

Many of us carry around class stereotypes about who belongs in Unitarian Universalist congregations—and we have all heard anecdotes. In May 2006 I was in Syracuse, New York, for a meeting of the St. Lawrence Foundation Board. This board gives out grants annually to theological schools and students. As we were leaving the meeting, I strolled toward my car chatting with another member of the board. He surveyed the parking lot and said, "It looks like there are a lot of Prius cars here. That must mean there are quite a few UUs staying at our hotel." He then pointed out the location of his own Subaru, but went on to say, "We once had a truck, and we drove into a UU parking lot. That was not good."

This reminds me of a story my wife Andrea, a multigenerational UU, tells about one of her brothers who went to church in Northampton, Massachusetts, for a while. Brian told the person he was talking to at social hour that he was a carpenter. The person automatically assumed Brian was not college-educated, which he is, and then directly asked him why he would ever come to a Unitarian Universalist church, since he was obviously not the right type of person. This person never learned that Brian grew up UU and has a sister, brother-in-law, cousin, and an uncle who are UU ministers.

These assorted stories carry the assumptions that a liberal thinking person's faith will not appeal to those who are not college-educated, work with their hands, drive pick-up trucks, or live more than twenty miles from an art museum. In fact, these assumptions may be simply untrue. Church members often feel the pressure to fit a stereotype, and those who are not college-educated are some-times afraid to admit it. While the class issue might have once been about money, family heritage, and privileged control, today it is more about a sense of educated cultural superiority.

Charles Vickery was a closeted gay minister who came from a middle class family from Pittsfield, Maine, where his father owned an insurance company. He once said,

> A church which has any trace of class or racial segregation or supernatural deity or a personal father who will shield people from life, should be destroyed. It has not the answer for our time. It kills man, rather than helping him grow.[38]

Much of our historical awareness about race and class comes from Mark Morrison-Reed, who wrote *Black Pioneers in a White Denomination*. He describes a split in the development of American religion into what he calls two American faiths: the religion of the middle class and the religion of the disinherited. He was invoking theologian H. Richard Niebuhr, author of *The Social Sources of Denominationalism*, who suggested that denominationalism follows social class. Middle class churches emphasize individual self-consciousness, personal salvation, and financial security. Morrison-Reed writes, "Often their [the liberal] vision was narrow and their understanding too limited to see beyond the status quo or to step beyond the narrow class appeal of the Unitarian Church."

The UUA Commission on Intergroup Relations reported that the mandate before the Unitarians was to fulfill their democratic spirit in developing a religious movement in which all may participate, without thought of racial or national origins.[39]

One of the central aspects of liberal religion is individualism, and so personal success, liberty, and salvation are central. But has its emphasis on individual fulfillment defined us in narrow demographic patterns which prevent us from building a broader community? The commission reported that those black people who became Unitarians were the educated, the cultured, and the prosperous.

Most Unitarian Universalists these days believe that everybody should have a fair chance and that everybody is equal. Yet these ideals of access and equality are not congruent with the realities of the lives of many Americans. In *The Trouble with Diversity: How We Learned to Love Identity and Ignore Inequality*, Walter Michaels explains that affirming diversity can lead us away from the true social inequalities that grip our nation. We embrace diversity because of our belief in individual freedom and end up trapped in identity politics. Michaels writes,

> A society free not only of racism, but of sexism and of heterosexism is a neoliberal utopia where all the irrelevant grounds for inequality (your identity) have been eliminated and whatever inequalities are left are therefore legitimated.[40]

So multiculturalism becomes a corporate management tool—as long as we feel liberated in our identity, then we have achieved salvation. We are ostensibly fully accepted and affirmed by the society in its current socio-economic stratification. As long as we succeed and are accepted, do the poor really matter any more? Further, as long as you don't display ill will toward the poor and homeless, then there are no grounds for attacking capitalism. It becomes a non-issue.

The affirmation of individuals and their freedom to be who they are has been wonderful and liberating, but it has only been so for those groups centered upon identity. So while each of the identity-based groups (such as women, blacks, gays and lesbians) feels affirmed, a broader liberation based on class disparities may be neglected. Our democratic, inclusive vision may achieve some diversity of color or sexual identity, but no economic, cultural, or educational diversity. We need to figure out how this universal, democratic message can be translated into a broader means of welcoming people. One of my students in a course I teach on polity once commented that the poor person who might fit in would be a downwardly mobile but college-educated ex-hippie— while the financially comfortable, pest control officer, who has no college education and several children, would not feel welcome. Where is the hospitality toward the second person? Can we cross our class divide?

Statistics support the fact that Unitarian Universalists are demographically separated from most Americans by wealth and education, and even place of residence. We want to grow in numbers in ways that will also reflect more class diversity, and wonder if this is possible. Even as we founded new congregations in green, leafy suburbs, we articulated a dream of being more diverse. The dream was realized for a time in Cleveland, and we all know some congregations today that seem to welcome a greater diversity of classes within their ranks. Congregations in places like Oakland, California, have persevered, survived, kept their historic building, and eventually flourished by affirming their neighborhood status. But they continue to be exceptions. At one time, UUA ministerial settlement forms asked if prospective candidates would be willing to serve in a city or in a rural setting but did not ask if we were willing to live in suburbia.

Thirty years ago at General Assembly, Victor Carpenter gave the James Luther Adams Lecture, "Urban Ministry: Wilderness and Wonderland." In that talk he said the city is the place where different people come together. He described the city as a liberating place where people are freed from the beliefs that blood, race, education, or income level are the only things that matter.[41] We live in a time where the gulfs that separate classes have grown even wider. We have a dream that we would grow and change as people and be spiritually richer if our churches truly lived out this democratic ideal that they have always envisioned but never enacted.

We know from our history in Britain and from our Universalist history in America that a liberal message can appeal to people who have fewer resources than most of our current members. In a paper written a few years ago, historian Charles Howe surveyed Unitarian Universalism in the South and spoke of our history serving as a challenge both for inclusivity and for perseverance in unreceptive environments.[42] Let us take up that challenge.

Theologically we have to dig deeper than the affirmation of self and our own achievements. Throughout our history our democratic ideal has often been bolstered by a theology, especially among Universalists, of a communitarian vision of one world, a heaven where all are equals—a classless place. Recently we have retreated from expressing a unified vision for Unitarian Universalism.

In the 1960s Unitarian Universalism was promoted as a syncretistic faith that drew upon all the world's religions in an effort to find what is common in all. We once saw world religions as a unified whole. In more recent times we seem to have embraced a more post-modernist view that celebrates diversity but fails to promote a singular vision. We celebrate how different we are but simultaneously fail to express any belief that might be construed as universal, as this would be condescending to an individual's or a faith's integrity. A remnant of this universal vision is our sixth Principle: "The goal of world community with peace, liberty, and justice for all." But what do we mean by that, and can we still express a common vision for our faith? We have always believed in the human capacity for change and improvement.

We have seen how our recent Unitarian Universalist ancestors achieved a certain degree of economic and educational status and then separated themselves from others in suburbs and away from the cities. Yet many of them remained concerned about how they could enact their religious message of one world, one common spirit uniting all people. They longed for true relationships with those from whom they were separated. They wanted to heal some of those class divisions. Historically that was sometimes done in a paternalistic manner, but the longing for oneness remained, so when our spiritual founder William Ellery Channing said, "I am a leveler," he was aware that our class separations must be bridged. Perhaps we need to broaden our understanding of who belongs among us. Maybe we are a thinking person's faith, but people in all classes think deeply and broadly. May our history teach us to live our faith in the world, so that each of us might come to say, "I am a leveler."[43]

Afterword

T HE SPRING 2010 cover story of the *UU World* poses the question: "Can We Change?" This book does not offer a definitive answer to that question, but lifts up historical examples of how Unitarians and Universalists called for a free faith that was meant to appeal to a wide diversity of people. The embodied reality was often neither inclusive nor egalitarian.

Today the denomination has made a commitment to create a faith that is both multicultural and multiracial. Juan M. Floyd-Thomas, in his book *The Origins of Black Humanism in America: Reverend Ethelred Brown and the Unitarian Church*, reminds us of the privileged heritage of those who have typically embraced our liberal faith. He reiterates Reinhold Niebuhr's claim that our faith is not a religious choice for the "disinherited, marginalized, and oppressed," but instead its adherents are "privileged, comfortable, and prosperous." He says that the great Unitarian historian Earl Morse Wilbur made presumptions about what types of people would "get" Unitarianism and endorsed the idea that it was a faith for the erudite and socially conscious. Others would not find it appealing.[1]

Floyd-Thomas tells the story of the Church of the Unitarian Brotherhood in Cincinnati. It was a storefront congregation founded in 1927 by William H. G. Carter, an African-American minister. While other Unitarian churches in greater Cincinnati knew about this congregation, none made any effort to make personal connections with the people or minister there. The best they could do was offer some old hymnals. Finally, the AUA's Lon Ray Call visited the church in 1938 but found that the neighborhood was poor and rowdy. Worse, two Unitarian ministers who had been invited to speak at the church said the congregation's response was "not very intelligent." In the end, Call said that he could not recommend Unitarian fellowship for Carter or subsidy for this new congregation. The brief history of this church soon ended.[2]

Today educators talk about different ways of measuring intelligence. I wish we could embrace different ways to be Unitarian Universalist. It is partly a matter of changing our perception of who is one of us. Rather than saying Carter was not one of us, let us imagine an affirmative response that this person discovered Unitarian Universalism and wanted to spread the faith at a storefront in Cincinnati.

Can we change? It will not be by denominational fiat or by a bunch of white liberals feeling guilty that their congregation is not diverse. It will require personal connections. It will require sharing power and control. It will require changed perceptions of status and education.

Recently two parishioners from Watertown visited a nearby UU congregation. They said that the focus on them as visitors seemed to be on whether they owned their own home or rented. The implied question was, Are you rich enough to be one of us? This is not the way to grow a diverse faith.

I think the historical examples from this book are useful in pointing the way to a new day for Unitarian Universalism. While

Cincinnati is one type of example, we are aware that Unitarianism in Britain brought in working class Methodists and Baptists, who longed for the affirmation and embrace of a loving God who saved all. Universalists in America drew from many different classes.

In the churches I have served in Massachusetts, the electrician and veteran in Palmer were as faithful as the professor and doctor in Milton. It would be a shame to lose the diversity we have even now. The problem is with our expectations, not with the faith itself. Change means we must broaden our expectations, and then make the dream a reality. The institutional goal of diversity and the theology of Universalism can only be realized through personal connection.

Acknowledgments

THIS BOOK IS A revised version of my 2008 Minns Lectures. I would like to thank all those who made both the lectures and this resulting publication a reality. Fayre Stephenson, a former intern of mine in Watertown and now the program director at Ferry Beach, originally suggested "class" as a topic for a summer conference during UU Heritage Week at Ferry Beach. This stimulated further research and conversations with colleagues. I also want to express my gratitude to the Minns Lectureship Committee, who were gracious and kind in all their support for me. I am especially grateful for their financial support of this book. Any book requires the helpful hand of those who manage archives and libraries. I want to acknowledge the help of John Hurley at the Unitarian Universalist Association and Fran O'Donnell at the Andover Harvard Theological Library. I want to thank the publications staff at the UUA, especially Editorial Director Mary Benard for encouraging me to reorganize and rewrite, and Editor Marshall Hawkins for editorial assistance and support. My wife, Rev. Andrea Greenwood, has more insights into UU history than I do, and I am grateful for the lost family time she indulges me with, but moreover for conversations that led ever deeper into the meaning of our faith. She may know more about English Unitarian history than any living person. Finally, I want to dedicate this book to my parents, who introduced me to many more class issues and their relevance to faith than they ever realized.

Notes

Introduction

1. Leonard Silk and Mark Silk, *The American Establishment* (Basic Books, Inc., 1980). For the history of Watertown, see Maud deLeigh Hodges, *Crossroads on the Charles: A History of Watertown, Massachusetts* (Watertown Free Public Library, 1980).
2. David Rankin, "Good News." (Sermon given at the First Parish of Lexington, Massachusetts, March 24, 1968.) Archival Files, First Parish of Watertown, Mass.
3. Tom Schade, "Hoping Their Hopes." (Sermon given at The First Unitarian Church of Worcester, Massachusetts, March 2010.) See: www.firstunitarian.com/memoarchive.html.
4. John Hurley, "Presentation at First Universalist Church—October 25, 2008." See www.firstuniv150.org/articles.
5. Rebecca Parker, "State of the School Report," Starr King School for the Ministry, October 16, 2009, p. 11.
6. Charles Capper, *Margaret Fuller, An American Romantic Life: The Private Years* (Oxford University Press, 1992), p. 75.

The British Challenge and American Beginnings

1. Anthony Lane, "Children's Tales," *The New Yorker* 82, no. 46. (January 22, 2007), p. 90.
2. Linda Lear, *Beatrix Potter: A Life in Nature* (St. Martin's Press, 2007), p. 38.
3. Ibid.

4. Frederick T. Wood, *A History of Underbank Chapel, Stannington* (J.W. Northend Ltd., 1944), p. 13.

5. Graham Hague and Judy Hague, *The Unitarian Heritage: An Architectural Survey* (P.B. Godfrey, 1986), pp. 19–20.

6. Earl Morse Wilbur, *A History of Unitarianism: In Transylvania, England, and America* (Beacon Press, 1945), pp. 249–250.

7. Ruth Watts, *Gender, Power and the Unitarians in England, 1760–1860* (Longman, 1998), p. 5.

8. Jenny Uglow, *The Lunar Men: Five Friends Whose Curiosity Changed the World* (Farrar, Straus and Giroux, 2002), pp. 52, 390, 451. See Andrea Greenwood, "British Unitarianism, Education and Class," (Paper given at Ferry Beach, Saco, Maine, August, 2006). See also Howard M. Wach, "Unitarian Philanthropy and Cultural Hegemony in Comparative Perspective: Manchester and Boston, 1827–1848," *Journal of Social History* 26 (1993), pp. 539–557. Wach suggests that the Unitarians in Manchester, England, identified with the anti-aristocratic impulses of radical Whiggery and were part of a middle-class effort to remake state and society. Boston Unitarians, on the other hand, supported efforts to rescue and reconstitute elite political authority. Brian Dolan in *Wedgwood, The First Tycoon* (New York, 2004, pp. 266–267) quotes George Courtauld, a British industrialist, who said that "the aim of business is to provide for the wants and comforts in the world." These religious dissenting industrialists believed in improving the standards of living and the moral worth of all their workers. As employers they held certain responsibilities, including developing programs such as conducting research to eliminate lead from glazes, starting schools for children, and training workers with new skills. Wedgwood was "determined to provide what he could for the community."

9. Watts, p. 6.

10. J. D. Bowers, *Joseph Priestley and English Unitarianism in America* (Pennsylvania State University Press, 2007), p. 201.

11. Leonard Smith, *The Unitarians: A Short History* (Lensden Publishing, 2006), p. 86.
12. Watts, pp. 163, 174–175, 182.
13. David L. Wykes, " 'Training Ministers Suited to the Wants of the Less Educated Classes': The Establishment of the Unitarian Home Missionary Board," *Transactions of the Unitarian Historical Society* (April 2005), pp. 615–616.
14. Smith, p. 90.
15. Stuart Andrews, *Unitarian Radicalism: Political Rhetoric 1770–1814* (Palgrave MacMillan, 2003), p. 99.
16. Joseph Priestley, as quoted in Andrews, p. 174
17. H. Richard Niebuhr, *The Social Sources of Denominationalism* (New American Library, 1975), pp. 30–31.
18. Edwin Scott Gausted, *The Great Awakening in New England* (Quadrangle Books, 1968), p. 99.
19. Alan Heimert, *Religion and the American Mind* (Harvard University Press, 1966), pp. vii–viii, 47.
20. William G. McLoughlin, *Revivals, Awakenings and Reform* (Little, Brown and Co., 1978), pp. 72–73.
21. Jonathan Mayhew, as quoted in Heimert, p. 170.
22. Jonathan Mayhew, "Men, Endowed with Faculties Proper for Discerning the Difference Betwixt Truth and Falsehood, and . . ." in *Seven Sermons* (Rogers and Fowle, 1749), p. 30.
23. Samuel Bigelow to Isaac Backus, April 9, 1774, Backus Papers, Andover Newton Theological School, Newton, Mass.
24. Nathaniel Stacy, *Memoirs of the Life of Nathaniel Stacy, Preacher of the Gospel of Universal Grace* (Abner Vedder, 1850), p. 106.
25. Mark W. Harris, *Among the Dry Bones: Liberal Religion in New Salem, Massachusetts: 1750–1850* (Unitarian Universalist Association, 1983), p. 24.
26. John Patrick Diggins, "Transcendentalism and the Spirit of Capitalism" in *Transient and Permanent: The Transcendentalist Movement*

and Its Contexts, Charles Capper and Conrad E. Wright, editors (Massachusetts Historical Society, 1999), pp. 238–239.

27. Olympia Brown, as quoted in *Olympia Brown: The Battle for Equality* by Charlotte Coté (Mother Courage Press, 1988), p. 130. (From a speech given in Rockford, Illinois.)

28. Olympia Brown, "Woman's Suffrage," (1888), in *Suffrage and Religious Principle: Speeches and Writings of Olympia Brown.*, Dana Greene, editor (Scarecrow Press, 1983), p. 111. See also Coté, *Olympia Brown*, pp. 129–131.

29. Laura Horton, "Lucy Barns's *The Female Christian:* A Universalist Treasure Rediscovered (Again)" in *The Unitarian Universalist Christian* 58, pp. 77–90.

Brahmin Culture for the Masses

1. Richard Eddy Sykes, "Massachusetts Unitarianism and Social Change," (Ph.D. diss., University of Minnesota, 1966), p. 173.

2. Henry Ware Jr., *Sober Thoughts on the State of the Times* (Isaac R. Butts, 1835), pp. 13–14.

3. Alpheus Harding to Charles Briggs, February 14, 1835, bMS 571/17, American Unitarian Association Letter Book, Andover Harvard Theological Library, Harvard Divinity School. See also Harris, *Among the Dry Bones*, pp. 145–146.

4. Peter S. Field, *The Crisis of the Standing Order* (University of Massachusetts Press, 1998), pp. 8, 9, 12, 75.

5. Charles Beecher, editor, *Autobiography, Correspondence, etc. of Lyman Beecher, D. D.*, Vol. 2 (Harper and Brothers Publisher, 1865), p. 110.

6. William H. Pease and Jane H. Pease, "Whose Right Hands of Fellowship? Pew and Pulpit in Shaping Church Practice," in *American Unitarianism, 1805–1865*, Conrad E. Wright, editor (Massachusetts Historical Society and Northeastern University Press, 1989), pp. 182, 185.

7. Ronald Story, *Harvard and the Boston Upper Class: The Forging of an Aristocracy, 1800–1870* (Wesleyan University Press, 1970), p. 4.

8. Judith Steen and Carolyn Swift, editors, *Georgianna: Feminist Reformer of the West, The Journal of Georgianna Bruce Kirby, 1852–1860* (Santa Cruz County Historical Trust, 1987), p. 7.

9. Story, pp. 7, 17.

10. Anne C. Rose, *Transcendentalism as a Social Movement, 1830–1850* (Yale University Press, 1981), pp. 19, 21.

11. Story, pp. 30, 80, 107.

12. Sykes, p. 159.

13. *Proceedings of a Meeting of Friends of Rev. John Pierpont and his Reply to the Charges of the Committee of Hollis Street Society* (S. N. Dickinson, 1839), p. 19.

14. Pease, pp. 195–201.

15. See "Bernard Whitman" by Peter Hughes at www25.uua.org/uuhs/duub/articles/bernardwhitman.html; Elizabeth D. Castner, *Tercentennial History of the First Parish in Waltham, Massachusetts, 1696–1996* (1998), pp. 305–306.

16. Hughes.

17. Sykes, pp. 153, 155.

18. Ibid., p. 158.

19. Octavius Brooks Frothingham, *Boston Unitarianism, 1820–1850: A Study of the Life and Work of Nathaniel Langdon Frothingham* (G.P. Putnam's Sons, 1890), p. 251.

20. Joseph Herring, "Arthur Buckminster Fuller," www25.uua.org/uuhs/duub/articles/arthurbuckminsterfuller.html.

21. Richard F. Fuller, *Chaplain Fuller: Being a Life Sketch of a New England Clergyman and an Army Chaplain* (Walker, Wise and Co., 1864), pp. 135, 129.

22. Ibid., pp. 165, 168.

23. Ann Douglas, *The Feminization of American Culture* (Alfred A. Knopf, 1977), pp. 281–282.

24. Ibid., pp. 298–300.

25. Sykes, pp. 138–139. See also "Seating the Meetinghouse in Early Massachusetts," by Robert J. Dinkin in *Material Life in America 1600–1860*, Robert Blair St. George, editor (Northeastern University Press, 1988), pp. 407–418.

26. Joseph Tuckerman, *On the Elevation of the Poor: A Selection From His Reports as Minister at Large in Boston* (Roberts Brothers, 1874), pp. 34–35.

27. Joseph Tuckerman, *Principles and Results of the Ministry at Large* (J. Munroe, 1838), p. 231.

28. Tuckerman, *On the Elevation*, pp. 27–28.

29. Arthur M. Schlesinger Jr., *A Pilgrim's Progress: Orestes A. Brownson* (Little, Brown and Co., 1966). Originally published in 1939, pp. 30, 102.

30. Richard Hofstadter, *Anti-Intellectualism in American Life* (Vintage, 1962).

31. George Ripley, as quoted in *American Transcendentalism, A History* by Phillip F. Gura (Hill and Wang, 2007), p. 141.

32. George Ripley, as quoted in *The American Transcendentalists*, Lawrence Buell, editor (The Modern Library, 2006), p. 104.

33. Charles Crowe, *George Ripley: Transcendentalist and Utopian Socialist* (University of Georgia Press, 1967), p. 121.

34. George Ripley to Ralph Waldo Emerson, as quoted in *Transcendentalism: A Reader* by Joel Myerson (Oxford University Press, 2000), p. 308.

35. Stanley Delano, *Brook Farm: The Dark Side of Utopia* (Harvard University Press, 2004), p. 161.

36. George Ripley, as quoted in Crowe, p. 197.

Universalism and a Classless Heaven

1. Charles A. Howe, "Cousins Twice Removed: Unitarians and Universalists in the South," *Unitarian Universalism: Selected Essays 1996* (Unitarian Universalist Ministers Association, 1996), p. 59.

Notes

2. Mark W. Harris, "Hosea Ballou's *Treatise* at 200," *The Unitarian Universalist Christian* 60, pp. 5–20.

3. Ibid. See also Stephen A. Marini, *Radical Sects of Revolutionary New England* (Harvard University Press, 1982).

4. George Rogers, *The Pro and Con of Universalism, Both as to Its Doctrine and Moral Bearings* (A.B. Grosh and Co., 1840), pp. 27–28.

5. William G. McLoughlin, *New England Dissent, 1630–1833: The Baptists and the Separation of Church and State*, Vol. 1 (Harvard University Press, 1971), p. 721.

6. McLoughlin, *Isaac Backus and the American Pietistic Tradition* (Little, Brown and Co., 1967), p. 177.

7. Russell E. Miller, *The Larger Hope: The First Century of the Universalist Church in America, 1770–1870* (Unitarian Universalist Association, 1979), p. 760; Historical Records Survey, *Inventory of Universalist Archives in Massachusetts* (Work Projects Administration, 1942), p. 241.

8. Marini, p. 98

9. Harris, *Among the Dry Bones*, pp. 112–113, 186–187.

10. Marini, pp. 98–99.

11. Ann Lee Bressler, *The Universalist Movement in America, 1770–1880* (Oxford University Press, 2001), p. 163.

12. John B. Buescher, *The Other Side of Salvation: Spiritualism and the Nineteenth-Century Religious Experience* (Skinner House Books, 2004), p. 143.

13. Ibid., p. 46; Hosea Ballou, "Feast of Knowledge," in *Sermons on Important Doctrinal Subjects* (G.W. Bazin, 1832), pp. 145–146.

14. Ernest Cassara, *Hosea Ballou: The Challenge to Orthodoxy* (Beacon Press and Universalist Historical Society, 1961), pp. 158–160; E. Brooks Holifield, *Theology in America: Christian Thought from the Age of the Puritans to the Civil War* (Yale University Press, 2003), p. 18.

15. Bressler, pp. 22–23; Sean Wilentz, *The Rise of American Democracy* (W.W. Norton & Co., 2005), pp. 282–285.

16. David E. Bumbaugh, "Reflections on Class in the History of Unitarianism, Universalism, and Unitarian Universalism," UUA General Assembly Address, 2000, p. 3.

17. Peter Hughes, "A Faith With Aspiration," *Journal of Liberal Religion* 3, no. 2 (Summer 2002), www.meadville.edu/LL_JournalLR_3_2.htm.

18. Carl Seaburg, *Inventing a Ministry, Four Reflections on the Life of a Colleague, Charles Vickery, 1920–1972* (Minns Lectureship Committee, 1992), pp. 47, 51.

19. Hughes, "Faith," p. 1.

20. Martha Hodes, *The Sea Captain's Wife: A True Story of Love, Race, and War in the Nineteenth Century* (W.W. Norton & Co., 2007), p. 94.

21. Ibid., pp. 92, 142, 154–155.

22. Ibid., pp. 92, 198.

23. Hughes, "Faith," p. 3.

24. George H. Williams, "American Universalism," *Journal of the Universalist Historical Society* 9, pp. 52–55; William Heighton, quoted in Bressler, p. 22.

25. See Harris, "Ballou's *Treatise.*"

26. Hosea Ballou and Joel Foster, *A Literary Correspondence* (William Butler, 1799), p. 27.

27. Mark Noll, *America's God: From Jonathan Edwards to Abraham Lincoln* (Oxford University Press, 2002), p. 153.

28. Hosea Ballou, "Gems of Thought," 1853. Vol. IV, bMS 366/2 (13), Andover Harvard Theological Library, p. 160.

29. Harris, *Among the Dry Bones*, pp. 73–74. See also Nathaniel Stacy, *Memoirs of the Life of Nathaniel Stacy, Preacher of the Gospel of Universal Grace* (A. Vedder, 1850), pp. 25–26.

30. Walter Donald Kring, *Henry Whitney Bellows: A History of the Unitarian Church of All Souls* Vol. II (Skinner House Books, 1979), pp. 447–448.

31. Anne Gertrude Sneller, *A Vanished World* (Syracuse University Press, 1964), p. 316.
32. Bressler, pp. 24, 28, 32; Ballou, *Treatise*, pp. 33–34.
33. Ballou, *Treatise*, pp. 34–35.
34. Ibid., pp. 193, 237.
35. Holifield, p. 230.
36. Williams, p. 77.
37. Bressler, pp. 7, 152.
38. John Murray, *The Life of Rev. John Murray* (A. Thompkins, 1844), pp. 185–186.

Scientific Salvation

1. Richard Hofstadter, *Social Darwinism in American Thought* (Beacon Press, 1955), p. 195. See also Gayle Williams, "David Starr Jordan," www25uua.org/uuhs/duub/articles/davidstarrjordan.html.
2. Hofstadter, p. 164.
3. David Starr Jordan, *The Blood of the Nations: A Study of the Decay of Races Through the Survival of the Unfit* (American Unitarian Association, 1902), pp. 25, 33.
4. David Starr Jordan, *The Heredity of Richard Roe, A Discussion of the Principles of Eugenics* (Beacon Press, 1911), Preface, pp. 153–154.
5. Jordan, *Blood of the Nations*, pp. 53, 57, 66; David Starr Jordan, *Life's Enthusiasms* (Beacon Press, 1906), pp. 51–52.
6. Hofstadter, pp. 17–18.
7. Horace Mann, "Twelfth Annual Report (1848) to the Massachusetts Board of Education," in *The Republic and the School: Horace Mann on the Education of Free Men*, Lawrence A. Cremin, editor (Teachers College Press, 1957), p. 87.
8. Michael D'Antonio, *The State Boys Rebellion* (Simon and Schuster, 2004), p. 6.
9. D'Antonio, p. 7; Hofstadter, p. 161.

10. D'Antonio, p. 9.
11. Paul A. Lombardo, *Three Generations, No Imbeciles: Eugenics, the Supreme Court, and Buck v. Bell* (Johns Hopkins University Press, 2008), pp. 160–162.
12. Ibid., p. 287.
13. Ibid., pp. 110, 167–170, 277–278.
14. Ian Dowbiggin, *A Merciful End: The Euthanasia Movement in Modern America* (Oxford University Press, 2003), p. 74.
15. Margaret Sanger, *An Autobiography* (Dover Publications Inc., 1971), reprint of 1938 edition, p. 375.
16. Russell E. Miller, *The Larger Hope: The Second Century of the Universalist Church in America, 1870–1970* (Unitarian Universalist Association, 1985), p. 468.
17. Christine Rosen, *Preaching Eugenics: Religious Leaders and the American Eugenics Movement* (Oxford University Press, 2004), p. 58.
18. Miller, *Second Century*, p. 734; Clarence Russell Skinner, "The Social Implications of Universalism," *The Annual Journal of the Universalist Historical Society* 5. Orig. pub. 1915, p. 104.
19. Rosen, p. 121.
20. Martin E. Marty, *Modern American Religion*, Vol. 2, *The Noise of Conflict, 1919–1941* (University of Chicago, 1991), p. 65.
21. Mason Olds, *American Religious Humanism* (Fellowship of Religious Humanists, 1996), p. 133.
22. Charles Francis Potter, *The Preacher and I: An Autobiography* (Crown Publishers Inc., 1951), pp. 300, 425, 427. See also Mark W. Harris, *Historical Dictionary of Unitarian Universalism* (Scarecrow Press, 2004), pp. 374–376.
23. Ibid., p. 396.
24. Ian Dowbiggin, "'A Rational Coalition': Euthanasia, Eugenics, and Birth Control in America, 1940–1970," in *The Journal of Policy History* 14, p. 223.
25. Dowbiggin, *A Merciful End*, p. 44.

26. "Dr. Potter Backs 'Mercy Killings,'" *New York Times*, February 3, 1936.

27. Dowbiggin, "A Rational Coalition," p. 234.

28. Charles Francis Potter, "A Message to America," Broadcast in the World of Religion Programs, June 25, 1933, by the National Broadcasting Company. www.infidel.org.

29. Dowbiggin, *A Merciful End*, p. 47.

30. Francis Greenwood Peabody, *Reminiscences of Present Day Saints* (The Riverside Press, 1927), p. 65.

31. Barton J. Bernstein, "Francis Greenwood Peabody: Conservative Social Reformer," *The New England Quarterly* 36, (Sept. 1963) p. 322.

32. Ibid., p. 320.

33. Ibid., p. 326.

34. Peabody, *Reminiscences*, p. 151.

35. Francis Greenwood Peabody, *Jesus Christ and the Social Question* (The Macmillan Co., 1900), p. 131.

36. Bernstein, p. 327.

37. Ibid., p. 320.

38. George H. Williams, "American Universalism, A Bicentennial Historical Essay," *Journal of the Universalist Historical Society* 9, pp. 52–56; Miller, *Second Century*, p. 735.

39. Hofstadter, pp. 167–168.

40. Olds, p. 167.

41. Clarence Russell Skinner. *A Religion for Greatness* (Universalist Publishing House, 1945), pp. 120–121.

A Faith for a Few

1. Ellen Tucker Emerson to Edith E. Forbes, *The Letters of Ellen Tucker Emerson*, Vol. 1, Edith E. W. Gregg, editor (Kent State University Press, 1982), p. 700.

2. James O'Connell, *Becoming Cape Cod* (University Press of New England, 2003), pp. 11–12.

3. Dorothy T. Spoerl, "Overview on Extension Practices in the American Unitarian Association, The Universalist Church of America, and the Unitarian Universalist Association" in *The Commission on Appraisal Report to the Trustees of the Unitarian Universalist Association on a Brief Look at the History of Extension* (Unitarian Universalist Association, 1978), p. 4.

4. Lon Ray Call, "A Research on Church Extension and Maintenance Since 1900—A Progress Report" (1946), American Unitarian Association. Department of Extension and Maintenance, Administrative Records, bMS11049, Andover Harvard Theological Library, Cambridge, Mass., p. 15.

5. Ibid., p. 26.

6. Lon Ray Call, "Report of the Department of Extension," May 1948, Unitarian Universalist Association. Inactive Minister File, 1825–1999, bMS 01446, p. 2.

7. Ibid., p. 6.

8. Lon Ray Call to George G. Davis, November 13, 1946, bMS 11052–3, American Unitarian Association, Department of Extension, Administrative Subject Files.

9. Dale DeWitt to Lon Ray Call, January 4, 1949, bMS 11052–3, American Unitarian Association, Department of Extension, Administrative Subject Files.

10. Lon Ray Call, "Shall Unitarians and Universalists Unite?" (1960), Unitarian Universalist Association, Inactive Minister Files, 1825–1999, bMS 01446, p. 5.

11. Robert Raible to George Spencer, November 7, 1971, Unitarian Universalist Association, Inactive Minister Files, 1825–1999, bMS 01446, Lon Ray Call.

12. Laile E. Bartlett, *Bright Galaxy: Ten Years of Unitarian Fellowships* (Beacon Press, 1960), pp. 62–63.

13. Lon Ray Call, "Organizational Guide, Aids and Suggestions for Establishing a Unitarian Fellowship in Your Community," (1954), American Unitarian Association, Department of Extension and Maintenance, Administrative Records, bMS11049, p. 3.

14. Munroe Husbands, "Organizing and Serving Unitarian Fellowships," Unitarian Fellowship Office, 1956, American Unitarian Association, Department of Extension and Maintenance, Administrative Records, bMS11049, p. 2.

15. "Unitarians Unite," 10, Report of the Commission on Planning and Review, October 1947, AUA.

16. Bartlett, p. 244.

17. Holley Ulbrich, *The Fellowship Movement: A Growth Strategy and Its Legacy* (Skinner House Books, 2008), p. 2.

18. Ibid., p. 67.

19. Bartlett, p. 68.

20. Commission on Appraisal, *Belonging: The Meaning of Membership* (Unitarian Universalist Association, 2001), pp. 64–67, 82.

21. Peter Richardson, *The Boston Religion* (Red Barn Publishing, 2003), p. 36.

22. Gerald Gamm, *Urban Exodus: Why the Jews Left Boston and the Catholics Stayed* (Harvard University Press, 1999), pp. 220–221.

23. Michael H. Frisch, *Town Into City* (Harvard University Press, 1972), p. 33.

24. *"Never Complete"* (1990), First Unitarian Universalist Church, Springfield, Mass., Unitarian Universalist Association Archives, Files on Churches: Springfield, Massachusetts.

25. Eleanor Herrick to Frederick May Eliot, June 28, 1953, UUA Archives, Springfield File.

26. Frederick May Eliot to Eleanor Herrick, July 1, 1953, UUA Archives, Springfield File.

27. Frederick May Eliot to Ernest H. Sommerfeld, July 7, 1953, UUA Archives, Springfield File.

28. Grant Butler to Ernest H. Sommerfeld, October 5, 1951, UUA Archives, Springfield File.
29. Eleanor Herrick to Frederick May Eliot, July 4, 1953, UUA Archives, Springfield File.
30. "Architectural, Historical, and Sociological Analysis of Springfield's Church of the Unity Building," *Springfield Sunday Republican*, March 5, 1961, 5E, UUA Archives, Springfield File.
31. Alice Harrison, Field Report, December 3, 1962, UUA Archives, Springfield File.
32. Berkeley Fellowship of Unitarian Universalists, www.bfuu.blogspot.com/2003/06/congregational-history.html. "Perhaps most relevant to the Berkeley Fellowship's core values was the fact that the Berkeley Fellowship families shared a commitment to remain in the heart of Berkeley."
33. Merv Hasselmann, "The First Unitarian Church of Berkeley: A History" (First Unitarian Church, 1981).
34. "The History of Unitarianism in Cleveland," (1958), UUA Archives, Church Files on Cleveland, Ohio, First Unitarian Church, p. 12.
35. Richard Wager, "Color-Blind Church," *Cleveland Plain Dealer*. Copy in UUA Archives, Church Files on Cleveland, Ohio, First Unitarian Church.
36. *UUA Now*, December 8, 1969, p. 6. Copy in UUA Archives, Church Files on Cleveland, Ohio, First Unitarian Church.
37. "New Congregation Proposal: Urban Hope Unitarian Universalist Congregation, Cleveland, Ohio," May 26, 1996. UUA Archives, Church Files on Cleveland, Ohio, First Unitarian Church.
38. Carl Seaburg, *Inventing a Ministry, Four Reflections on the Life of a Colleague, Charles Vickery, 1920–1972* (Minns Lectureship Committee, 1992), p. 75.
39. Mark Morrison-Reed, *Black Pioneers in a White Denomination* (Skinner House Books, 1980), pp. 145–146.

40. Walter Benn Michaels, *The Trouble With Diversity: How We Learned to Love Identity and Ignore Inequality* (Henry Holt and Company, 2006), p. 75.
41. Victor H. Carpenter, *Stations of the Spirit* (Sunflower Ink, 1990), pp. 31–48.
42. Charles A. Howe, "Cousins Twice Removed: Unitarians and Universalists in the South," *Unitarian Universalism, Selected Essays 1996* (Unitarian Universalist Ministers Association, 1996), p. 65.
43. See Howard M. Wach, "Unitarian Philanthropy and Cultural Hegemony in Comparative Perspective: Manchester and Boston, 1827–1848," *Journal of Social History* 26 (1993), pp. 539–557.

Afterword

1. Paul Rasor, "Can Unitarian Universalism Change?" *UU World* 24, no. 1 (Spring 2010), pp. 33–38; Juan M. Floyd-Thomas, *The Origins of Black Humanism in America: Reverend Ethelred Brown and the Unitarian Church* (Palgrave MacMillan, 2008) p. 63.
2. Juan M. Floyd-Thomas, *The Origins of Black Humanism in America: Reverend Ethelred Brown and the Unitarian Church* (Palgrave MacMillan, 2008) p. 74.

Resources

Andrews, Stuart. *Unitarian Radicalism: Political Rhetoric 1770–1814.* New York: Palgrave MacMillan, 2003.

Ballou, Hosea. *A Treatise on Atonement.* Boston: Skinner House Books, 1986. First published in 1805.

Bowers, J. D. *Joseph Priestley and English Unitarianism in America.* University Park, Pa.: The Pennsylvania State University Press, 2007.

Bressler, Ann Lee. *The Universalist Movement in America, 1770–1880.* New York: Oxford University Press, 2001.

Buell, Lawrence, editor. *The American Transcendentalists.* New York: The Modern Library, 2006.

Buescher, John B. *The Other Side of Salvation: Spiritualism and the Nineteenth-Century Religious Experience.* Boston: Skinner House Books, 2004.

Bumbaugh, David E. "Reflections on Class in the History of Unitarianism, Universalism, and Unitarian Universalism." Address given at the Unitarian Universalist General Assembly, Nashville, Tenn., 2000.

Capper, Charles. *Margaret Fuller, An American Romantic Life: The Private Years.* New York: Oxford University Press, 1992.

Commission on Appraisal. *Belonging: The Meaning of Membership.* Boston: Unitarian Universalist Association, 2001.

Crowe, Charles. *George Ripley: Transcendentalist and Utopian Socialist.* Athens, Ga.: University of Georgia Press, 1967.

D'Antonio, Michael. *The State Boys Rebellion*. New York: Simon and Schuster, 2004.

Delano, Stanley F. *Brook Farm: The Dark Side of Utopia*. Cambridge, Mass.: Harvard University Press, 2004.

Dolan, Brian. *Wedgwood: The First Tycoon*. New York: Viking Penguin, 2004.

Dowbiggin, Ian. *A Merciful End: The Euthanasia Movement in Modern America*. New York: Oxford University Press, 2003.

Field, Peter S. *The Crisis of the Standing Order*. Amherst, Mass.: University of Massachusetts Press, 1998.

Floyd-Thomas, Juan M. *The Origins of Black Humanism in America: Reverend Ethelred Brown and the Unitarian Church*. New York: Palgrave MacMillan, 2008.

Freeberg, Ernest. *The Education of Laura Bridgman: First Deaf and Blind Person to Learn Language*. Cambridge, Mass.: Harvard University Press, 2001.

Gamm, Gerald. *Urban Exodus: Why the Jews Left Boston and the Catholics Stayed*. Cambridge, Mass.: Harvard University Press, 1999.

Gura, Phillip F. *American Transcendentalism, A History*. New York: Hill and Wang, 2007.

Hague, Graham and Judy Hague. *The Unitarian Heritage: An Architectural Survey*. Sheffield, England: P.B. Godfrey, 1986.

Harris, Mark. *Among the Dry Bones: Liberal Religion in New Salem, Massachusetts*. Springfield, Mass.: Connecticut Valley District, Unitarian Universalist Association, 1981.

———. *Historical Dictionary of Unitarian Universalism*. Lanham, Md.: Scarecrow Press, 2004.

Hodes, Martha. *The Sea Captain's Wife: A True Story of Love, Race, and War in the Nineteenth Century*. New York: W.W. Norton & Co., 2007.

Hofstadter, Richard. *Social Darwinism in American Thought.* Boston: Beacon Press, 1955.

Holifield, E. Brooks. *Theology in America: Christian Thought from the Age of the Puritans to the Civil War.* New Haven: Yale University Press, 2003.

Howe, Charles A. "Cousins Twice Removed: Unitarians and Universalists in the South," *Unitarian Universalism: Selected Essays 1996.* Boston: Unitarian Universalist Ministers Association, 1996.

Hughes, Peter. "A Faith With Aspiration," *Journal of Liberal Religion* 3, no. 2 (Summer 2002). www.meadville.edu/LL_JournalLR_3_2.htm.

Lear, Linda. *Beatrix Potter: A Life in Nature.* New York: St. Martin's Press, 2007.

Lombardo, Paul A. *Three Generations, No Imbeciles: Eugenics, the Supreme Court, and Buck v. Bell.* Baltimore: The Johns Hopkins University Press, 2008.

Marini, Stephen A. *Radical Sects of Revolutionary New England.* Cambridge, Mass.: Harvard University Press, 1982.

Marty, Martin E. *Modern American Religion*, Vol. 2 *The Noise of Conflict, 1919–1941.* Chicago: University of Chicago Press, 1991.

Michaels, Walter Benn. *The Trouble With Diversity: How We Learned to Love Identity and Ignore Inequality.* New York: Henry Holt and Company, 2006.

Morrison-Reed, Mark. *Black Pioneers in a White Denomination*, Third Edition. Boston: Skinner House Books, 1994.

Noll, Mark. *America's God: From Jonathan Edwards to Abraham Lincoln.* New York: Oxford University Press, 2002.

Rasor, Paul. *Faith Without Certainty: Liberal Theology in the 21st Century.* Boston: Skinner House Books, 2005.

———. "Can Unitarian Universalism Change?" *UU World* 24, no. 1, (Spring 2010), pp. 33–38.

Richardson, Peter. *The Boston Religion*. Rockland, Maine: Red Barn Publishing, 2003.

Rose, Anne C. *Transcendentalism as a Social Movement, 1830–1850*. New Haven: Yale University Press, 1981.

Rosen, Christine. *Preaching Eugenics: Religious Leaders and the American Eugenics Movement*. New York: Oxford University Press, 2004.

Sanger, Margaret. *An Autobiography*. New York: Dover Publications, Inc., 1971 (reprint of 1938 edition).

Schultz, Ronald. *The Republic of Labor: Philadelphia Artisans and the Politics of Class, 1720–1830*. New York: Oxford University Press, 1993.

Silk, Leonard, and Mark Silk. *The American Establishment*. New York: Basic Books, Inc., 1980.

Smith, Leonard. *The Unitarians: A Short History*. Cumbria, England: Lensden Publishing, 2006.

Story, Ronald. *Harvard and the Boston Upper Class: The Forging of an Aristocracy, 1800–1870*. Middletown, Conn.: Wesleyan University Press, 1980.

Uglow, Jenny. *The Lunar Men: Five Friends Whose Curiosity Changed the World*. New York: Farrar, Straus and Giroux, 2002.

Watts, Ruth. *Gender, Power and the Unitarians in England, 1760–1860*. New York: Longman, 1998.

Williams, Gayle. "David Starr Jordan," www.25uua.org/uuhs/duub/articles/davidstarrjordan.html.

Index

Index

Index